Jenny Craig's
SIMPLE PLEASURES
Recipes To Nourish Body and Soul

Jenny Craig's
SIMPLE PLEASURES
Recipes To Nourish Body and Soul

Oxmoor
House.

Library of Congress Catalog Card Number: 98-66931
ISBN: 0-8487-1838-0

Manufactured in the United States of America
First Printing 1998

Be sure to check with your health-care provider before making
any changes in your diet.

Editor-in-Chief: Nancy Fitzpatrick Wyatt
Senior Foods Editor: Katherine M. Eakin
Senior Editor, Editorial Services: Olivia Kindig Wells
Art Director: James Boone

Jenny Craig's Simple Pleasures

Editor: Cathy A. Wesler, R.D.
Contributing Editor: Lisa Talamini Jones, R.D.
Associate Art Director: Cynthia R. Cooper
Senior Designer: Melissa Clark
Copy Editor: Shari K. Wimberly
Editorial Assistant: Lauren Brooks
Director, Test Kitchens: Kathleen Royal Phillips
Assistant Director, Test Kitchens: Gayle Hays Sadler
Test Kitchen Home Economists: Julie Christopher, Natalie E. King,
    Iris Crawley O'Brien, Jan A. Smith
Senior Photographer: Jim Bathie
Photographers: Ralph Anderson, Van Chaplin, Brit Huckabay,
    Becky Luigart-Stayner, Howard L. Puckett, Charles Walton IV
Senior Photo Stylist: Kay E. Clarke
Photo Stylists: Virginia R. Cravens, Cindy Manning Barr
Publishing Systems Administrator: Rick Tucker
Director, Production and Distribution: Phillip Lee
Associate Production Manager: Vanessa Cobbs Richardson
Production Assistant: Faye Porter Bonner

Cover: *Pink Grapefruit and Champagne Sorbet* (page 42)
Back cover: *Malibu Brownie Torte* (page 86)

Dedication

This book is dedicated to the person with whom I share simple pleasures every day, my husband and partner in all things that matter, Sid Craig.

And to you, our clients. May your enthusiasm and personal effort enable you to develop a healthy relationship with food and discover the joy of an active lifestyle. One choice at a time, you'll find ways to renew, replenish, and balance your life with its many demands.

Contents

Malibu Brownie Torte (page 86)

*Fettuccine with Shrimp and
Roasted Red Peppers (page 41)*

Dear Readers,

Fifteen years ago, my husband, Sid, and I created a program called Jenny Craig. It began as a mission to help people realize their weight goals. It has evolved into so much more.

Weight is a reflection of lifestyle—a lifestyle in balance. With all our roles and responsibilities, it's easy to see how daily stressors can throw our lives out of kilter and cause us to resort to unhealthy ways to cope. That's why it has been so rewarding to see our clients not just lose weight but restore their sense of balance as well.

How do our clients measure their success? In simple ways, like enjoying the tastes of all foods, consciously choosing the ones that nourish both the body and soul . . . by embracing a variety of physical activities, being mindful of the need to be invigorated one day, relaxed the next . . . by calmly responding to daily challenges, even welcoming them as opportunities to grow.

Over the years, Sid and I have grown to appreciate the value of simplicity, too. Living near the ocean, we can enjoy quiet walks along the beach, just the two of us. Or we'll have the grandchildren over for a rambunctious splash in the surf. In food, our tastes turn to the simple as well—fresh, uncomplicated, and healthfully prepared. That's not to say we don't indulge in a piece of good chocolate or a glass of fine wine—in moderation. For us, eating in this simple, balanced way has become a real pleasure.

Simple pleasures—that's what these recipes are about. Each one has been chosen for the beauty of its ingredients, the richness of its flavors, and the ease of its preparation. All are low in fat; simply choose the ones with colors, tastes, textures, and aromas that call out to your senses.

Think of this book as a guide to healthy indulgence. Find ways to savor not just the food, but the other things that can nourish you as well. Take five minutes each day to pamper yourself. The perfect pear, a scented candle, or a single set of yoga stretches—let simple acts of pleasure empower you to live the life you deserve!

Jenny Craig

The Pleasures of Balance

Life Is an Act
of Balance

*Stop the world, I want to get off! I need to take a break, go
on vacation, escape now. . . . Sound familiar?*

In today's complicated and fast-paced world, we juggle many roles,
constantly trading the urgency of job, childcare, and eldercare
responsibilities on an as-needed basis. Work at the office blends into
work in the home, stretching a work week well past 40 hours. Meanwhile, cellular phones, pagers, e-mail, voice mail, and fax machines make
us accessible 24 hours, every day. No wonder it seems there's no time to
relax and rejuvenate.

Stress: Life Out of Balance

Stress is the body and mind's response to outside people, places, and
events. You've felt the symptoms—anxiety, a pounding heart, headaches,
fatigue, and muscle tension. High stress increases our risk for high blood
pressure and heart disease, sets us up for depression, and even lowers our
immunity. And for many of us, stress is the trigger to overeat.

Learning to recognize the physical and mental signals of stress (see
box below) is the first step to restoring balance. Once you tune into your
mind and body's response to life's demands you will discover healthful
and satisfying alternatives. Perhaps one of the most important things to
remember is that you have choices.

Learn To Ride the Wave

Stress can be overwhelming if you view it
as something that happens to you. One way
to keep your balance is to remind yourself
that stress is just your reaction to what happens in your life. You have options. Instead
of reacting negatively to stress, respond by
nourishing yourself, both physically and
spiritually, in healthier ways.

Think about the feelings associated with
your tension and anxiety. As you become
more aware of these feelings, you'll be able
to minimize your reactions and maintain
your sense of balance.

stress signals

Body Signals	Mind Signals
Increased breathing rate	*Fear*
Increased perspiration	*Resentment*
Increased heart rate	*Irritability*
Headaches	*Anxiety*
Backaches	*Depression*
Neck aches	*Anger*
Upset stomach	*Forgetfulness*
Insomnia	*Negativity*
Fidgeting	*Confusion*

Replenish Your Spirit

When the pace gets feverish, do you tend to go on autopilot, eliminating even the simplest of pleasures because they seem to be a luxury in the midst of the turmoil?

Actually, it's the simple pleasures that can help you hold on to your well-being. An early morning walk, a home-cooked meal, a favorite comic strip—these are the things that can replenish your spirit and bolster your strength in times of stress. Look inward, and choose the ones that will truly nourish your body and soul.

relax and rejuvenate

Light scented candles

Burn incense

Enjoy bath oils

Use lotions

Soak in a tub

Dance

Read a novel or a book of meditations

Listen to relaxation tapes

Peruse books of art

Swing in a hammock

Walk the dog

Tend a garden

Sip sparkling water

Keep a Healthy Perspective

When you're late for work because of a traffic jam, does it throw off your whole day? Next time you get upset over trivial things that are out of your control, ask yourself:

How important is it? Very few issues are truly life-threatening, so this one is probably not worth the energy of your worry.

What can I do to control it right now? If you stay objective, you'll know what you can change and what you can't. Accept both, and you'll more easily move on with your day.

The Goal Is Progress, not Perfection

Be realistic in your pursuit of balance. Some days, you'll eat more healthfully, other days you'll be more active, and at times you'll manage stress better than others. Life is never perfectly balanced.

Compare balance to a beam suspended on a rope. While you can't keep the beam still, you can master the art of standing on it gracefully as it gently tilts from side to side.

Be Gentle With Yourself

How do you react to stress now? Is the way you choose giving you what you need? If your answer is no, resist the urge to judge yourself. Instead, honor your new awareness, and try one of the healthier responses at left.

Indulge in Simplicity

- *Reduce weekend and late evening hours.*
- *Limit important tasks to five or less.*
- *Clear your desk of extra papers and add a single photo or bud vase.*
- *Pare down your wardrobe with stress-free neutrals.*
- *Delegate, delegate, delegate!*

. . . At Home

- *Combine shopping and errands in one trip.*
- *Limit social engagements and make them memorable.*
- *Combine physical activities with family time.*
- *Reduce magazine subscriptions to just a few.*
- *Give back-of-the-closet clothes to charity.*

. . . In the Kitchen

- *Buy prepackaged individual grocery items.*
- *Make one-dish weekday meals.*
- *Simplify entertaining by planning potlucks for 8 instead of dinner parties for 50.*
- *Prepare a recipe using just its key ingredients.*
- *Use easy, full-flavored cooking techniques.*
- *Accent the dish with a single herb or spice.*
- *Finish off a meal with the sensual, such as whole berries, dark chocolate, and sorbet.*

How do you indulge in simplicity? To indulge usually means to enjoy in excess. To simplify is to strip away the excess. It's true that most of us long for a simpler life. Yet it seems self-indulgent to let go of important details. How is it possible to live authentically and responsibly, yet still indulge in simple pleasures and simpler choices? Once again, it's a matter of balance.

Do What You Love First

Balance isn't about saving the best until last. It's about building your day around the things that matter most. Let your personal priorities be the foundation, a source of inner strength.

When you don't have time to do everything on your schedule, just be sure to do the things that energize and fulfill you. The rest will fall into place.

Keep in Touch—With Yourself

The simple act of asking yourself what you need can be a powerful tool for harmony. Often, it's just the basics—food, water, rest, movement—that get lost among life's distractions. And it's the lack of these basics that clouds our judgment and turns minor issues into major challenges.

What do you need, right now? Maybe a bite to eat, a sip of water, a short nap, or a leisurely stroll. When you indulge in the simple act of self-care, you nurture your mind, body, and spirit. You'll find that once you take the time to do these things, you'll have more energy and hopefully a brighter outlook on your day.

Minimize To Maximize

When it comes to decorating, home management, office organization, or even cooking, the trend is toward minimalism. Everyone is looking to reduce clutter—at work, at home, and in the kitchen. The payoff: more time to indulge in healthy pleasures.

What Enriches Your Life Most?

Your spouse

Your children

Personal growth

Spirituality

Physical activity

Arts and entertainment

Hobbies

Traveling

Enjoy This Moment

How often do you allow yourself to enjoy the moment—this very moment—without the distraction of yesterday or tomorrow? Busy lifestyles lead us to rush from one activity to the next with barely a glimpse, let alone an experience, of what occurred.

The practice of mindfulness, moment-by-moment awareness, fully engages all your senses so you can be present for everything in your life. It can be as formal as daily meditation or as simple as just paying attention to what is happening—right now.

What is the benefit of mindfulness? You'll be able to experience people, places, and events in a more conscious, objective way. Instead of automatically reacting to a situation, mindfulness gives you a space in time to respond with a healthier choice. That's why it's such a powerful tool for restoring life balance.

Mindfulness holds an even greater gift. It instantly simplifies and illuminates whatever you are doing. It links your physical senses—sight, hearing, taste, smell, touch—with your intuitive ones. Try this and you'll find the experience is transforming. Even something as ordinary as eating becomes extraordinary if done slowly and mindfully. Mindfulness takes simple pleasures to the next level.

Start With the Breath

A simple way to begin being mindful is to attend to your breathing habits. Think of your breath as your center, and breathing as a way to quiet your mind, especially in times of stress. Take a moment and try this quick version of mindful breathing. Afterwards, notice how relaxed yet alert you feel!

Next time you take a walk, focus on your breath. Then add your posture or stride to your focus. Notice the difference awareness makes in your experience. Walking not only burns calories, but it can also be very renewing if done mindfully.

Savor "Empty" Moments

Do you *save* time or do you *savor* it? When you're lucky enough to capture a few extra minutes, how do you use them? Do you tackle an extra task? Or do you relish the moment—take a break to refresh and

renew? Next time you're waiting at a stop sign, standing in line at the bank, or on hold on the phone, pause, take one deep, relaxing breath, and let your mind run free.

Where else in your day can you find a few extra minutes for a mini-meditation? No matter how busy you are, give yourself at least 15 minutes of "me" time every day. You might use this time to plan for the coming day or just to relax. You'll find it a lot easier to dig in again once you've taken some time for yourself.

Eat in the Moment

Instead of eating on the run, take time to taste your meal, paying attention to the colors, flavors, textures, and aromas and enjoying every aspect as a nourishing experience. Tune into your sense of physical hunger as well. Listen to your body's natural signals—it will make the experience far more satisfying.

Take a breath. Sip some water. Appreciate the beauty of the food. Take a single bite. Notice the flavors, the "mouth-feel." Swallow slowly before your next bite. Pause midmeal to check your appetite. Listen to your body. Finish when you are satisfied, not stuffed.

Nourish the Body

5 Self-Care Essentials

- *Mindful breathing*
- *Rejuvenating rest*
- *Cleansing water*
- *Conscious eating*
- *Invigorating movement*

5 Things To Ask When You're Hungry

- *What is it I need?*
- *Is it food to nourish me?*
- *Is it a walk to re-energize me?*
- *Is it a talk to express my emotions?*
- *Or is it a long, deep breath that will restore my calm?*

5 Body-Nourishing Benefits of Physical Activity

- *Reduces heart risk—lowers blood cholesterol and triglyceride levels*
- *Helps manage diabetes—improves blood sugar and blood cholesterol levels*
- *Helps prevent osteoporosis—helps build bone mass before age 30, and helps maintains it after age 30*
- *Helps prevent colon cancer—increases regularity, reducing exposure to carcinogens*
- *Helps prevent breast cancer—reduces body fat and estrogen exposure*

5 Ways To Feed Your Body's Metabolism

- *Eat mini-meals, 5 to 6 per day. Overall, you'll burn more calories.*
- *Build your meals around carbohydrates, as your body spends more to digest them.*
- *Lift light weights and you'll build calorie-burning muscle.*
- *Interject intervals—short speed-ups in your intensity—and you'll burn up more calories.*
- *Switch activities—it costs more calories for your body to retrain.*

5 Natural Ways To Ease Into Menopause

- *Boost your calcium intake from 2 to 5 servings a day of milk or other dairy products to keep bones strong.*
- *Enjoy soy. Rich in anti-hot flash phyto-estrogens, soybeans and tofu also contain genestein, a potential risk reducer for breast cancer.*
- *Ask your doctor about vitamin E which may lessen symptoms and reduce postmenopause risks for heart disease.*
- *Focus on lowering fat, an easy way to prevent the typical post-40 weight gain.*
- *Get physical! Activity causes endorphins, natural mood enhancers, to pulse through your system, acting to neutralize the anxiety and depression that may follow hormone changes.*

Take Five . . .

Five minutes, that is, to nourish yourself

every day with simple pleasures. Five

minutes equals 300 seconds—300

moments for you to:

- *Spark your self-awareness*

- *Stimulate your senses*

- *Savor a new food*

- *Try a new low-fat cooking technique*

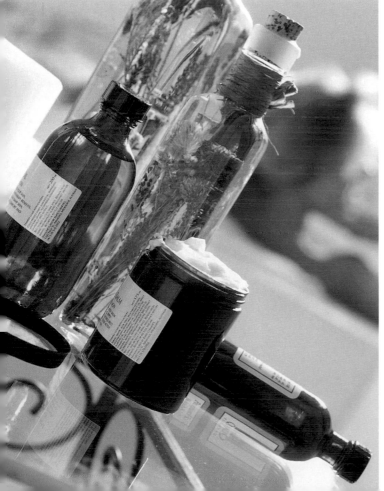

- *Enhance your health*

- *Relax your mind*

- *Soothe your soul*

Don't underestimate the power of 5!

Nourish the Soul

take five

5 Mentally Centering Activities
- *Dance*
- *Golf*
- *Yoga*
- *Tai Chi*
- *Meditation*

5 Comfort Spices
- *Ginger*
- *Cinnamon*
- *Vanilla*
- *Nutmeg*
- *Cloves*

5 Aromas to Soothe
- *Chamomile*
- *Eucalyptus*
- *Lavender*
- *Peppermint*
- *Almond*

5 Ways to Create an Eating Oasis
- *Turn off the TV*
- *Turn on the answering machine*
- *Turn up some music*
- *Eliminate distractions*
- *Relax and enjoy!*

5 Nurturing Foods
- *Casseroles*
- *Breads, scones, and muffins*
- *Soups and stews*
- *Pies, cobblers, and crisps*
- *Chocolate anything!*

The Pleasures of Healthy Eating

Five Ways to Simplify Mealtime

Start your balanced lifestyle with great-tasting meals as the foundation. But don't be intimidated by the thought of planning a menu. After all, a menu is simply three or four items that go together to make up a meal. There isn't any rule that says you must start from scratch and prepare a recipe for each item. We've used this premise in planning our menus, beginning on page 27.

Whether preparing a single recipe or combining them into a menu, you'll want to take shortcuts in the kitchen, giving you more time for the important people in your life. As you prepare a meal for family and friends, keep in mind these shortcuts. You'll find they will quickly become routine steps in your everyday meal preparation.

•**Use heavy-duty, zip-top plastic bags for easy cleanup**.
    Marinate meat or poultry in the bag, turning bag occasionally to completely coat the food.
    When roasting meat, pour slightly cooled pan drippings into the bag. Let the fat rise to the top. Then snip off one bottom corner, and pour out the fat-free broth. The fat will stay in the plastic bag.
    Use a bag to drizzle melted chocolate over desserts. First, use the microwave to melt the chocolate in the bag. Then snip off one bottom corner to form a small hole, and squeeze.

•**Spray measuring cups and spoons with vegetable cooking spray before measuring** honey or peanut butter. It helps these sticky ingredients come out easily.

•**Use kitchen shears to chop or mince herbs** right into a glass measuring cup, eliminating a cutting board.

•**Use a graduated measuring spoon or cup**. It's a spoon (or cup) that adjusts for different measurements so you don't have as many utensils to clean up afterward.

•**Preheat the oven before you assemble the recipe** when baking, broiling, or roasting. If you forget, it will take the oven 10 to 15 mnutes to reach the specified temperature.

MENUS

Fettuccine with Shrimp and
Roasted Red Peppers (page 41)

COMFORT LUNCH COMBO

Spicy Tomato-Corn Chowder

Glorified Grilled Cheese

Fresh apples

Spicy Tomato-Corn Chowder

Vegetable cooking spray
2 teaspoons roasted garlic-flavored vegetable oil
1 (10-ounce) package frozen whole-kernel corn, thawed
1½ teaspoons dried basil
1 (14¼-ounce) can no-salt-added chicken broth
1 (10¾-ounce) can reduced-fat, reduced-sodium tomato soup
½ teaspoon hot sauce
¼ teaspoon salt
¼ teaspoon pepper
Nonfat sour cream (optional)

Coat a large saucepan with cooking spray; add oil, and place over medium-high heat until hot. Add corn and basil; sauté 2 minutes.

Add broth and next 4 ingredients to saucepan. Bring to a boil; cover, reduce heat, and simmer 20 minutes. Top each serving with sour cream, if desired. Yield: 4 (1-cup) servings.

•**Per Serving:** Calories 140   Carbohydrate 24.8g   Protein 3.4g   Fat 4.0g
Fiber 2.4g   Cholesterol 0mg   Sodium 385mg   **Exchanges:** 1½ Starch,
1 Vegetable, 1 Fat

**Lunch
on the table in
30 minutes.**

1. Prepare chowder.

2. While chowder simmers, prepare sandwiches.

Glorified Grilled Cheese

⅓ cup Neufchâtel cheese, softened
½ teaspoon dried basil
8 (1-ounce) slices white or whole wheat bread
4 (¾-ounce) slices fat-free sharp Cheddar cheese
4 (¾-ounce) slices fat-free mozzarella cheese
1 tablespoon plus 1 teaspoon reduced-calorie margarine, softened
  Vegetable cooking spray

Combine Neufchâtel cheese and basil, stirring well. Spread cheese mixture evenly over one side of 4 bread slices. Place cheese slices over cheese mixture; top with remaining bread slices.

Spread margarine evenly over both sides of sandwiches. Place in a sandwich press or hot skillet coated with cooking spray. Cook until bread is lightly browned and cheese melts. Serve immediately. Yield: 4 servings.

•**Per Serving**: Calories 283 Carbohydrate 33.7g Protein 17.7g Fat 8.4g
Fiber 1.1g Cholesterol 22mg Sodium 898mg **Exchanges**: 2 Very Lean Meat, 2 Starch, 2 Fat

HOT, HEARTY & VEGETARIAN

Grecian Stuffed Potatoes

Spinach-Orange Salad

Peanut Butter Crunch Cookies

Grecian Stuffed Potatoes

**Lunch
on the table in
55 minutes.**

1. Bake potatoes in the oven or microwave until done.

2. While potatoes bake, prepare cookies.

3. Toss together ingredients for the salad.

4. Combine ingredients for potato topping, and serve.

4 (6-ounce) baking potatoes
1 (15-ounce) can no-salt-added garbanzo beans, drained
¼ cup plus 2 tablespoons water
¼ cup plus 1 tablespoon fresh lemon juice, divided
1½ teaspoons no-salt-added Greek seasoning, divided
½ teaspoon salt, divided
3 cups diced tomato
3 tablespoons sliced ripe olives
¼ teaspoon pepper
½ cup crumbled reduced-fat feta cheese

Scrub potatoes; prick each several times with a fork. Bake at 400° for 45 minutes or until done.

Position knife blade in food processor bowl; add beans, water, ¼ cup lemon juice, ½ teaspoon Greek seasoning, and ¼ teaspoon salt. Process 1 minute or until smooth. Combine remaining 1 tablespoon lemon juice, 1 teaspoon seasoning, and ¼ teaspoon salt; add tomato, olives, and pepper, stirring well.

Cut a lengthwise slit in top of each potato. Press ends of each potato toward center, pushing pulp up. Top evenly with bean mixture and tomato mixture; sprinkle with cheese. Yield: 4 servings.

•**Per Serving:** Calories 364   Carbohydrate 66.3g   Protein 15.5g   Fat 5.9g
Fiber 8.1g   Cholesterol 6mg   Sodium 645mg   **Exchanges:** 2 Lean Meat,
3 Starch, 1 Vegetable

Spinach-Orange Salad

6 cups torn fresh spinach
1 purple onion, sliced into rings
1 orange, peeled and cut into wedges
½ cup fat-free olive oil vinaigrette

Combine first 3 ingredients in a medium bowl, and toss well. Drizzle vinaigrette over salad mixture, and toss to combine. Yield: 4 (1½-cup) servings.

•**Per Serving**: Calories 68   Carbohydrate 14.6g   Protein 3.3g   Fat 0.4g
Fiber 5.9g   Cholesterol 0mg   Sodium 390mg   **Exchanges**: 3 Vegetable

Peanut Butter Crunch Cookies

3 cups corn flakes cereal
½ cup light-colored corn syrup
3 tablespoons sugar
⅓ cup reduced-fat creamy peanut butter

Place cereal in a large bowl; set aside. Combine syrup and sugar in a saucepan. Bring to a boil over medium-high heat; cook 1 minute. Remove from heat; stir in peanut butter.

Working quickly, pour peanut butter mixture over cereal; toss lightly to coat. Drop by heaping tablespoonfuls onto wax paper. Let stand at room temperature until firm. Store in an airtight container. Yield: 26 cookies.

•**Per Cookie**: Calories 55   Carbohydrate 10.4g   Protein 1.1g   Fat 1.2g
Fiber 0.1g   Cholesterol 0mg   Sodium 62mg   **Exchange**: 1 Starch

PACIFIC RIM ROAST

Indonesian Pork Tenderloin

Hot Sesame Spaghetti

Fresh orange wedges

Fortune cookies

Hot tea

Indonesian Pork Tenderloin

1 (1-pound) pork tenderloin
2 tablespoons low-sodium soy sauce
2 tablespoons reduced-fat creamy peanut butter
1 teaspoon dried crushed red pepper
2 cloves garlic, minced
   Vegetable cooking spray
¼ cup pineapple preserves

Trim fat from tenderloin. Combine soy sauce and next 3 ingredients, stirring well. Spread soy sauce mixture over tenderloin. Place on a rack in a roasting pan coated with cooking spray. Insert meat thermometer into thickest part of tenderloin, if desired.

Bake, uncovered, at 375° for 30 minutes. Brush tenderloin with preserves. Bake 10 additional minutes or until meat thermometer registers 160°, basting often with preserves. Let stand 10 minutes before slicing. Yield: 4 servings.

•**Per Serving**: Calories 247   Carbohydrate 17.5g   Protein 26.7g   Fat 7.3g
Fiber 3.2g   Cholesterol 79mg   Sodium 327mg   **Exchanges**: 3 Lean Meat, 1 Fruit

---

**Dinner
on the table in
50 minutes.**

1. Prepare and cook the tenderloin.

2. Cut oranges into wedges.

3. Cook the vegetables for the pasta, and bring water to a boil.

4. Cook the spaghetti when the tenderloin is removed from the oven.

5. Combine the spaghetti and chopped vegetables; toss and serve.

Hot Sesame Spaghetti

    Vegetable cooking spray
  2 teaspoons hot chile oil, divided
2½ cups coarsely chopped broccoli flowerets
  1 cup diced sweet red pepper
  ½ cup chopped green onions
1½ teaspoons minced garlic
  8 ounces spaghetti, uncooked
  1 tablespoon sesame seeds, lightly toasted
  ½ teaspoon salt

Coat a large nonstick skillet with cooking spray; add 1 teaspoon oil. Place over medium-high heat until hot. Add broccoli and next 3 ingredients; sauté until vegetables are crisp-tender.

Cook pasta according to package directions, omitting salt and fat; drain well. Toss with remaining 1 teaspoon oil. Add broccoli mixture, sesame seeds, and salt; toss well. Yield: 6 (1-cup) servings.

•**Per Serving**: Calories 181 Carbohydrate 32.2g Protein 6.5g Fat 3.1g
Fiber 2.5g Cholesterol 0mg Sodium 209mg **Exchanges**: 1½ Starch,
1 Vegetable, 1 Fat

SOUTHERN SUPPER

Cajun-Spiced Catfish

Parslied potatoes

Steamed broccoli

Cheddar Drop Biscuits

Oven-Fried Peach Pies

Cajun-Spiced Catfish

**Supper
on the table in
25 minutes.**

1. Quarter potatoes, and cook them in boiling water to cover for 15 minutes.

2. While the potatoes cook, make the biscuits.

3. Top the fish with the seasoning mixture. Cook the broccoli in the microwave while the fish is broiling.

4. Toss the potatoes with 2 teaspoons of melted margarine and fresh parsley just before serving.

5. Pop the pies into the oven as you sit down to eat.

2 tablespoons reduced-calorie margarine, melted
1 teaspoon dried basil
1 teaspoon dried thyme
1 teaspoon paprika
1 teaspoon black pepper
1 teaspoon ground red pepper
½ teaspoon salt
⅛ teaspoon garlic powder
4 (4-ounce) farm-raised catfish fillets
  Vegetable cooking spray

Combine first 8 ingredients in a small bowl.

Place fish on rack of a broiler pan coated with cooking spray. Brush fish with margarine mixture. Broil 5½ inches from heat (with electric oven door partially opened) 7 minutes or until fish flakes easily when tested with a fork. Yield: 4 servings.

•**Per Serving**: Calories 170   Carbohydrate 1.4g   Protein 20.9g   Fat 8.8g
Fiber 0.5g   Cholesterol 66mg   Sodium 420mg   **Exchanges**: 3 Lean Meat

Cheddar Drop Biscuits

  2 cups reduced-fat biscuit and baking mix
½ cup (2 ounces) shredded reduced-fat sharp Cheddar cheese
¾ cup skim milk
    Vegetable cooking spray
  2 tablespoons reduced-calorie margarine, melted
¼ teaspoon garlic powder
½ teaspoon dried parsley flakes, crushed

Combine baking mix and cheese in a bowl; make a well in center of mixture. Add milk, stirring just until dry ingredients are moistened.

Drop dough by rounded tablespoonfuls, 2 inches apart, onto a baking sheet coated with cooking spray. Bake at 450° for 8 minutes. Combine margarine, garlic, and parsley; brush over biscuits. Yield: 1 dozen.

•**Per Biscuit**: Calories 106 Carbohydrate 15.0g Protein 3.4g Fat 3.5g
Fiber 0.3g Cholesterol 3mg Sodium 291mg **Exchanges**: 1 Starch, ½ Fat

Oven-Fried Peach Pies

  1 cup drained canned peaches in light syrup, chopped
  3 tablespoons sugar, divided
¾ teaspoon ground cinnamon, divided
  1 tablespoon all-purpose flour
  1 (10-ounce) can refrigerated buttermilk biscuits
    Butter-flavored vegetable cooking spray

Combine peaches, 2 tablespoons sugar, and ½ teaspoon cinnamon. Sprinkle flour over work surface. Place biscuits on floured surface. Roll each to a 4½-inch circle. Place 1 heaping tablespoon peach mixture over half of each circle. Brush edges of circles with water; fold in half. Seal edges by pressing with a fork. Place on an ungreased baking sheet; coat with cooking spray. Combine remaining 1 tablespoon sugar and ¼ teaspoon cinnamon; sprinkle over pies. Bake at 375° for 10 minutes. Yield: 10 pies.

•**Per Pie**: Calories 107 Carbohydrate 19.9g Protein 2.2g Fat 2.6g
Fiber 0.4g Cholesterol 0mg Sodium 281mg **Exchanges**: 1 Starch, ½ Fruit

DINNER ALFRESCO

Fettuccine with Shrimp and
Roasted Red Peppers

Italian tossed salad

Dinner rolls

Grapefruit and
Pink Champagne Sorbet

Fettuccine with Shrimp and Roasted Red Peppers

1½ pounds jumbo shrimp, peeled
1 pound fresh asparagus spears
1 tablespoon olive oil
4 cloves garlic, pressed
⅓ cup fresh basil leaves, sliced into ribbons
1 (7.25-ounce) jar roasted red peppers, sliced
2 tablespoons capers, drained
1 teaspoon cornstarch
¾ cup fat-free chicken broth
2 tablespoons lemon juice
2 tablespoons dry white wine
4 cups cooked fettuccine (cooked without salt and fat)
   Freshly ground pepper (optional)

Peel shrimp, and devein, if desired, leaving tails intact. Snap off tough ends of asparagus; cut diagonally into 2-inch pieces. Steam 5 minutes or until crisp-tender.

Place oil in a saucepan over medium heat. Add garlic; sauté until tender. Add shrimp; cook for 3 minutes or until pink. Remove shrimp. Add asparagus, basil, red peppers, and capers to pan; heat thoroughly. Combine cornstarch and broth; add to pan. Cook, stirring occasionally, 5 minutes or until thickened. Stir in lemon juice and wine.

Place pasta in a bowl. Add shrimp and vegetable mixture; toss. Sprinkle with freshly ground pepper, if desired. Yield: 4 servings.

•**Per Serving:** Calories 432   Carbohydrate 48.3g   Protein 37.8g   Fat 8.6g
Fiber 4.2g   Cholesterol 199mg   Sodium 643mg   **Exchanges:** 3 Lean Meat,
2 Starch, 3 Vegetable

> **Dinner
> on the table in
> 60 minutes.**
>
> **1.** Prepare the sorbet.
>
> **2.** Wash mixed salad greens. Shake dry; cover and chill.
>
> **3.** Shred ¼ cup fresh Parmesan cheese, and set aside.
>
> **4.** Prepare fettuccine and shrimp recipe.
>
> **5.** Just before serving, toss greens with fat-free Italian dressing, and sprinkle with Parmesan cheese.

Pink Grapefruit and Champagne Sorbet

 1 large pink grapefruit
 2 cups pink grapefruit juice cocktail
 1 cup dry champagne
¼ cup sugar
    Grapefruit rind curls (optional)

Grate rind from pink grapefruit, and set aside. Carefully peel and section grapefruit, removing white membrane.

Position knife blade in food processor bowl; add grapefruit sections. Process until finely chopped. Add grapefruit juice and grapefruit rind; process until smooth.

Pour grapefruit mixture into freezer can of a 2-quart hand-turned or electric freezer. Add champagne and sugar; stir well. Freeze according to manufacturer's instructions. Let ripen 1 hour, if desired. Scoop sorbet into individual dessert bowls; garnish with grapefruit rind curls, if desired. Serve immediately. Yield: 4½ cups.

•**Per ½-cup Serving:** Calories 79   Carbohydrate 10.9g   Protein 0.3g
Fat 0.0g   Fiber 0.1g   Cholesterol 0mg   Sodium 4mg   **Exchange:** 1 Fruit

*Gone are the days when making frozen desserts took an afternoon—
and lots of turns at the crank. New electric and hand-turned
freezers have reduced the prep time and the mess. The one thing that
hasn't changed is the great homemade taste.*

ROMANTIC INTERLUDE

Veal in Lime Cream Sauce

Roasted Garlic and
Onion Linguine

Steamed Sugar Snap peas

Blushing Pears in Chocolate
Sauce

White wine

Veal in Lime Cream Sauce

**Dinner
on the table in
75 minutes.**

1. Roast the onion and garlic for the pasta dish.

2. After onion and garlic have been roasting for 30 minutes, brown the veal.

3. Process the garlic mixture.

4. Boil the water for the linguine, and let it cook while you prepare the cream sauce. Add the veal to the sauce.

5. Just before serving, steam the peas, and heat the rolls.

   1 pound veal cutlets (¼ inch thick)
  ¼ teaspoon salt
  ¼ teaspoon freshly ground pepper
      Butter-flavored vegetable cooking spray
   2 tablespoons fresh lime juice
   2 tablespoons dry white wine
   1 tablespoon plus 1 teaspoon all-purpose flour
  ½ cup canned low-sodium chicken broth
  ⅔ cup evaporated skimmed milk
  ½ teaspoon lime zest

Sprinkle veal cutlets with salt and pepper. Coat a large nonstick skillet with cooking spray; place over medium-high heat until hot. Add cutlets, and cook 1 minute on each side or until browned. Remove from skillet; set aside, and keep warm.

Add lime juice and wine to skillet; cook over high heat 1 minute or until mixture is reduced by half. Combine flour, broth, and milk; stir well. Add to lime juice mixture. Cook over medium heat, stirring constantly, 5 minutes or until thickened and bubbly. Return cutlets to skillet; cook until thoroughly heated. Transfer to a serving platter. Sprinkle with lime zest, and serve immediately. Yield: 4 servings.

•**Per Serving:** Calories 218   Carbohydrate 8.1g   Protein 31.0g   Fat 6.1g
Fiber 0.1g   Cholesterol 102mg   Sodium 282mg   **Exchanges:** 4 Lean Meat,
½ Starch

Roasted Garlic and Onion Linguine

2 small onions (about ½ pound)
1 small head garlic
  Olive oil-flavored vegetable cooking spray
¼ cup grated Parmesan cheese
¼ cup canned no-salt-added chicken broth
2 teaspoons olive oil
½ teaspoon cracked pepper
¼ teaspoon salt
12 ounces linguine, uncooked

Peel onions, and cut each into 8 wedges. Gently peel outer skin from garlic and discard. Cut off and discard top one-fourth of garlic head. Place onion and garlic, cut sides up, in center of a piece of heavy-duty aluminum foil; coat with cooking spray. Fold foil over onion and garlic, sealing tightly. Bake at 350° for 1 hour or until onion and garlic are soft. Remove from oven, and let cool.

Remove and discard skin from garlic. Scoop out garlic pulp with a small spoon. Position knife blade in food processor bowl; add garlic pulp, onion, and cheese. Pulse 5 times or until combined. Add broth and next 3 ingredients to garlic mixture. Process until mixture is finely chopped. Set aside.

Cook pasta according to package directions, omitting salt and fat; drain. Add garlic mixture; toss lightly. Serve immediately. Yield: 8 (¾-cup) servings.

•**Per Serving**: Calories 198   Carbohydrate 35.9g   Protein 7.1g   Fat 2.7g
Fiber 1.6g   Cholesterol 2mg   Sodium 125mg   **Exchanges**: 2 Starch,
1 Vegetable

TECHNIQUE

Peel the papery outer skin from the head of garlic. Cut off the top fourth of the head.

Place the peeled garlic and onion in the center of the foil, and coat with cooking spray. Seal foil, and bake for 1 hour. Remove the skin from garlic.

Blushing Pears in Chocolate Sauce

4 medium-size firm pears (about 1 ½ pounds)
2 tablespoons unsweetened orange juice
3 cups blush wine
1 ½ cups cranberry-raspberry juice cocktail
¼ cup powdered sugar
1 tablespoon plus 1 teaspoon unsweetened cocoa
1 teaspoon cornstarch
½ cup water
1 teaspoon vanilla extract

Peel pears; remove core from bottom end, leaving stem end intact. Slice ¼ inch from base of pears to sit flat. Brush with orange juice.

Combine wine and cranberry-raspberry juice in a large saucepan; bring to a boil. Place pears, stem end up, in pan. Cover, reduce heat, and simmer 15 minutes or just until pears are tender. Remove pears from liquid with a slotted spoon. Discard liquid.

Meanwhile, combine sugar, cocoa, and cornstarch in a saucepan. Gradually add water; stir until smooth. Cook, stirring constantly, over medium heat until slightly thickened. Remove from heat; stir in vanilla.

Spoon 1 tablespoon chocolate sauce onto each of 4 dessert plates; place pears on sauce. Drizzle 1 tablespoon sauce over each pear. Yield: 4 servings.

•**Per Serving**: Calories 197   Carbohydrate 48.5g   Protein 1.5g   Fat 0.9g
Fiber 3.7g   Cholesterol 0mg   Sodium 19mg   **Exchanges**: ½ Starch, 3 Fruit

• • • • • • • • • • • • •

For a perfect whole pear presentation, core pears from the
bottom, cutting to, but not through, the stem end.

APPETIZERS & BEVERAGES

Shrimp Canapés (page 58) and
Minted Orange-Lemon Fizz (page 61)

Red Bean Hummus with
Pita Wedges

PREP: 12 MINUTES

3 cloves garlic

1 (16-ounce) can red beans, drained

2 tablespoons fresh lime juice

2 teaspoons sesame oil

¼ teaspoon ground cumin

3 (6-inch) pita bread rounds

Position knife blade in food processor bowl. Drop garlic through food chute with processor running; process 3 seconds or until garlic is minced. Add beans and next 3 ingredients; process until smooth.

Separate each pita bread round into 2 rounds; cut each into 8 wedges. Serve hummus with pita wedges. Yield: 24 appetizer servings (serving size: 1 tablespoon dip and 2 pita wedges).

•**Per Serving**: Calories 47   Carbohydrate 8.2g   Protein 1.7g   Fat 0.6g
Fiber 1.4g   Cholesterol 0mg   Sodium 49mg   **Exchange**: ½ Starch

Red beans give hummus (a Middle Eastern dip
made with garbanzo beans) a new twist. Like traditional
hummus, this dip has a powerful garlic punch.

Artichoke and Green Chile Dip

PREP: 12 MINUTES   COOK: 26 MINUTES

⅔ cup nonfat mayonnaise

½ cup plain low-fat yogurt

1 (14-ounce) can artichoke hearts, drained and chopped

1 (4-ounce) can chopped green chiles, drained

¼ cup plus 2 tablespoons freshly grated Parmesan cheese

¼ teaspoon garlic powder

¼ teaspoon hot sauce

  Vegetable cooking spray

2 tablespoons freshly grated Parmesan cheese

Combine mayonnaise and yogurt in a medium bowl, stirring until smooth.

Add artichoke hearts and next 4 ingredients, stirring well. Spoon mixture into a 1-quart baking dish coated with cooking spray. Bake, uncovered, at 350° for 25 minutes.

Sprinkle with 2 tablespoons Parmesan cheese. Broil 5½ inches from heat (with electric oven door partially opened) 1½ minutes or until lightly browned. Serve with whole wheat toast points, breadsticks, unsalted crackers, or Melba rounds. Yield: 2¾ cups.

•**Per Tablespoon:** Calories 13 Carbohydrate 1.7g Protein 0.7g Fat 0.4g Fiber 0.1g Cholesterol 1mg Sodium 78mg **Exchange:** Free

An artichoke is in the thistle group of the sunflower family.
The part we eat is actually the plant's flower bud.
Artichokes are available fresh (whole), canned (hearts and
bottoms), or frozen (quartered).

Cheddar-Jack Cheese Ball

Cheddar-Jack Cheese Ball

PREP: 8 MINUTES   CHILL: 2 HOURS

½ cup Neufchâtel cheese, softened
2 tablespoons plain nonfat yogurt
½ cup (2 ounces) shredded reduced-fat Cheddar cheese
½ cup (2 ounces) shredded reduced-fat Monterey Jack cheese
1 teaspoon minced onion
1 teaspoon prepared horseradish
½ teaspoon Dijon mustard
⅛ teaspoon ground red pepper
2 tablespoons nutlike cereal nuggets
1½ tablespoons chopped fresh parsley
48 fat-free crackers

Combine Neufchâtel cheese and yogurt, stirring until smooth. Add Cheddar cheese and next 5 ingredients; stir well. Cover and chill at least 2 hours.

Shape cheese mixture into a ball. Wrap cheese ball in wax paper, and chill.

Combine cereal nuggets and parsley. Roll cheese ball in cereal mixture just before serving. Serve with fat-free crackers. Yield: 1 cup.

•**Per 1 Tablespoon Spread and 3 Crackers**: Calories 71   Carbohydrate 6.7g
Protein 4.2g   Fat 3.0g   Fiber 0.1g   Cholesterol 10mg   Sodium 138mg
Exchanges: ½ Medium-Fat Meat, ½ Starch

Crabmeat and Bacon Cups

PREP: 25 MINUTES   CHILL: 1 HOUR

    2 slices turkey bacon, cooked and crumbled
  $\frac{1}{2}$ pound fresh crabmeat, drained and flaked
  $\frac{1}{4}$ cup nonfat sour cream
  $\frac{1}{4}$ cup nonfat mayonnaise
$1\frac{1}{2}$ teaspoons fresh or frozen chopped chives
  $\frac{1}{4}$ teaspoon pepper
    2 (2.1-ounce) packages frozen miniature phyllo shells, thawed

Combine first 6 ingredients, stirring well. Cover and chill thoroughly. To serve, spoon crabmeat mixture into phyllo shells. Yield: 30 appetizers.

•**Per Appetizer:** Calories 35   Carbohydrate 3.2g   Protein 2.3g   Fat 1.3g
Fiber 0.0g   Cholesterol 8mg   Sodium 69mg   **Exchange:** ½ Starch

No need to purchase more expensive lump crabmeat for this recipe; save lump crab for salads and dishes requiring large pieces of meat. You can purchase regular crabmeat for these cups; regular (flaked) crabmeat includes all the meat from the body portion of the crab, excluding lump meat.

Peppered Tuna Bruschetta

PREP: 18 MINUTES   COOK: 10 MINUTES

1½ tablespoons olive oil, divided
4 (4-ounce) fresh tuna steaks
1 teaspoon freshly ground pepper
Olive oil-flavored vegetable cooking spray
1 (12-ounce) jar roasted red peppers in water
1 tablespoon chopped fresh tarragon
1 tablespoon fresh lemon juice
2 large cloves garlic, divided
30 (½-inch-thick) slices French baguette

Brush 1½ teaspoons olive oil evenly over tuna steaks. Sprinkle pepper over both sides of tuna, pressing pepper into tuna.

Coat grill rack with cooking spray; place on grill over medium-hot coals (350° to 400°). Place tuna on rack; grill, covered, 4 minutes on each side or until fish flakes easily when tested with a fork.

Flake tuna in a medium bowl. Drain red peppers, reserving liquid. Chop enough peppers to measure ¾ cup. Reserve remaining peppers and liquid for another use. Add chopped peppers, remaining 1 tablespoon olive oil, tarragon, and lemon juice to tuna, stirring lightly. Finely chop 1 clove garlic; add to tuna mixture. Set aside.

Lightly coat both sides of bread slices with cooking spray. Cut remaining 1 clove garlic in half; rub bread slices with cut sides of garlic. Arrange bread slices in a single layer on a baking sheet. Bake at 350° for 10 minutes or until lightly browned, turning once. Spoon tuna mixture evenly over bread slices. Yield: 30 appetizers.

•**Per Appetizer**: Calories 61   Carbohydrate 6.4g   Protein 4.4g   Fat 1.7g
Fiber 0.3g   Cholesterol 6mg   Sodium 78mg   **Exchange**: ½ Starch

White Chili Snackers

White Chili Snackers

PREP: 36 MINUTES   COOK: 5 MINUTES

    2 (4-ounce) packages roast-flavored chicken breast halves
    1 (15-ounce) can Great Northern beans, drained
  ¼ teaspoon ground cumin
  20 (3-inch) crackerbread rounds (or water crackers)
  ½ cup tomatillo salsa
  ½ cup (2 ounces) shredded reduced-fat Monterey Jack cheese
      Cherry tomato wedges (optional)
      Fresh cilantro leaves (optional)

Broil chicken according to package directions; let cool slightly. Shred chicken, and set aside.

Position knife blade in food processor bowl; add beans and cumin. Process 1½ minutes. Spread mixture over crackers; top with salsa and chicken. Sprinkle with cheese. Place on a baking sheet; bake at 400° for 5 minutes. If desired, garnish with tomato and cilantro. Yield: 20 appetizers.

•**Per Appetizer**: Calories 52   Carbohydrate 6.5g   Protein 4.5g   Fat 1.0g
Fiber 0.8g   Cholesterol 7mg   Sodium 147mg   **Exchange**: ½ Starch

Citrus-Marinated Shrimp and Scallops

PREP: 15 MINUTES   MARINATE: 30 MINUTES   COOK: 4 MINUTES

1 pound unpeeled large fresh shrimp
¼ cup frozen orange juice concentrate, thawed and undiluted
3 tablespoons honey
2 tablespoons water
1 tablespoon finely chopped green onion
1 tablespoon chopped fresh basil
½ pound bay scallops
   Vegetable cooking spray
3 cups shredded fresh spinach

Peel and devein shrimp, leaving tails intact.

Combine orange juice concentrate and next 4 ingredients in a large heavy-duty, zip-top plastic bag; add shrimp and scallops. Seal bag, and shake until seafood is well coated. Marinate in refrigerator 30 minutes, turning bag occasionally.

Remove shrimp and scallops from marinade, discarding marinade. Coat rack of a broiler pan with cooking spray. Place shrimp and scallops on rack; broil 5½ inches from heat (with electric oven door partially opened) 4 minutes or until done.

Place ½ cup spinach on each individual serving plate. Arrange shrimp and scallops on spinach. Yield: 6 appetizer servings.

•**Per Serving**: Calories 134   Carbohydrate 15.2g   Protein 16.4g   Fat 0.9g
Fiber 1.2g   Cholesterol 95mg   Sodium 179mg   **Exchanges**: 2 Very Lean Meat, 1 Fruit

Citrus-Marinated Shrimp and Scallops

Shrimp Canapés

PREP: 25 MINUTES   CHILL: 2 HOURS

12 unpeeled medium-size fresh shrimp
½ cup plus 1 teaspoon dry white wine, divided
½ cup canned no-salt-added chicken broth
2 fresh dillweed sprigs
6 (1-ounce) slices whole wheat bread
¼ cup light process cream cheese
1½ teaspoons minced fresh dillweed
   Fresh dillweed sprigs (optional)

Peel and devein shrimp, leaving tails intact, if desired. Combine ½ cup wine, broth, and 2 dillweed sprigs in a medium saucepan. Bring to a boil; add shrimp, and cook 3 to 4 minutes or until shrimp turn pink. Transfer shrimp and liquid to a bowl. Cover and chill thoroughly.

Cut whole wheat bread slices into 12 rounds with a 2-inch biscuit cutter. Reserve remaining bread pieces for another use. Place bread rounds on a baking sheet. Broil 5½ inches from heat (with electric oven door partially opened) 1 minute on each side or until lightly toasted.

Combine cream cheese, minced dillweed, and remaining 1 teaspoon wine. Spread cheese mixture evenly over one side of bread rounds. Remove shrimp from liquid; discard liquid. Place one shrimp on each bread round. Garnish with fresh dillweed sprigs, if desired. Yield: 12 appetizers. *(pictured on page 47)*

•**Per Appetizer**: Calories 30   Carbohydrate 2.7g   Protein 2.6g   Fat 1.0g
Fiber 0.2g   Cholesterol 18mg   Sodium 69mg   **Exchange**: Free

Oriental Vegetable Wontons

PREP: 16 MINUTES   COOK: 3 MINUTES

¼ cup rice wine vinegar
2 tablespoons low-sodium soy sauce
½ teaspoon garlic powder
¼ teaspoon ground ginger
¼ cup chopped fresh broccoli
¼ cup chopped cabbage
2 tablespoons chopped onion
2 tablespoons chopped fresh mushrooms
2 tablespoons fresh bean sprouts
1 teaspoon garlic powder
12 fresh or frozen wonton skins, thawed
Vegetable cooking spray

Combine first 4 ingredients, stirring well; set aside.

Position knife blade in food processor bowl; add broccoli and next 5 ingredients. Process until mixture is minced, scraping sides of processor bowl once.

Place vegetable mixture evenly on top corner of each wonton skin. Fold top point of wonton skin over filling; tuck point under filling. Roll once toward center, covering filling and leaving about 1 inch unrolled at bottom of skin. Moisten remaining corners with water; bring corners together, and overlap, pressing ends together to seal securely.

Cook wontons in boiling water 3 minutes or until tender. Drain; coat wontons with cooking spray, and arrange on 4 serving plates. Serve with vinegar mixture. Yield: 4 appetizer servings (serving size: 3 wontons).

•Per Serving. Calories 92   Carbohydrate 16.7g   Protein 3.2g   Fat 0.9g
Fiber 0.7g   Cholesterol 2mg   Sodium 338mg   **Exchange:** 1 Starch

Hawaiian Crush

PREP: 5 MINUTES

1¾ cups guava nectar

¾ cup water

1 (12-ounce) can frozen pineapple juice concentrate, thawed and undiluted

¼ teaspoon coconut extract

1 (33.8-ounce) bottle club soda, chilled

Combine first 4 ingredients in a large pitcher, stirring well. Cover and chill, if desired.

Just before serving, stir in club soda. Serve over crushed ice. Yield: 8 (1-cup) servings.

•**Per Serving**: Calories 110   Carbohydrate 27.2g   Protein 0.5g   Fat 0.0g
Fiber 0.5g   Cholesterol 0mg   Sodium 28mg   **Exchanges**: 2 Fruit

· · · · · · · · · · · · · ·

*Guava nectar is available in bottles in the juice section of
your grocery store. You'll find its refreshing flavor
reminiscent of pineapple and lemon.*

Minted Orange-Lemon Fizz

PREP: 20 MINUTES   CHILL: 1 TO 3 HOURS

1¼ cups water
⅔ cup sugar
½ cup tightly packed mint leaves
1 tablespoon grated orange rind
¾ cup unsweetened orange juice
¾ cup fresh lemon juice
2 cups lemon-flavored sparkling water, chilled
Fresh mint sprigs (optional)

Combine 1¼ cups water and sugar in a small saucepan; cook over medium heat, stirring constantly, until sugar dissolves. Remove from heat, and let cool completely.

Combine sugar mixture, ½ cup mint leaves, orange rind, orange juice, and lemon juice. Cover and chill.

Pour mixture through a wire-mesh strainer into a pitcher, discarding mint and orange rind. Just before serving, stir in sparkling water. Serve over ice. Garnish with fresh mint sprigs, if desired. Yield: 5 (1-cup) servings. *(pictured on page 47)*

•**Per Serving:** Calories 128   Carbohydrate 33 6g   Protein 0.4g   Fat 0.0g
Fiber 0.1g   Cholesterol 0mg   Sodium 21mg   **Exchanges:** 2 Fruit

Caramel-Nut Coffee Coolers

PREP: 5 MINUTES   CHILL: 1 HOUR

2½ cups brewed coffee
 3 tablespoons fat-free caramel-flavored syrup
 ½ cup refrigerated fat-free hazelnut-flavored nondairy
       coffee creamer
 ¼ cup frozen reduced-calorie whipped topping, thawed
 2 teaspoons fat-free caramel-flavored syrup

Combine coffee and 3 tablespoons caramel syrup, stirring until syrup dissolves. Stir in creamer; cover and chill.

Pour coffee mixture evenly into four glasses. Top each serving with 1 tablespoon whipped topping; drizzle evenly with 2 teaspoons syrup. Serve immediately. Yield: 4 (¾-cup) servings.

•**Per Serving:** Calories 134   Carbohydrate 28.9g   Protein 0.3g   Fat 0.6g
Fiber 0.0g   Cholesterol 0mg   Sodium 56mg   **Exchanges:** 2 Fruit

Caramel Hot Cocoa

PREP: 2 MINUTES   COOK: 6 MINUTES

 1 tablespoon sugar
 1 tablespoon unsweetened cocoa
1¾ cups skim milk
 2 tablespoons caramel ice cream topping

Combine sugar and unsweetened cocoa in a small saucepan; stir in skim milk and caramel ice cream topping. Cook, stirring constantly, over medium heat until mixture is thoroughly heated and caramel topping dissolves. Serve immediately. Yield: 2 (1-cup) servings.

•**Per Serving:** Calories 163   Carbohydrate 31.5g   Protein 8.4g   Fat 0.7g
Fiber 0.0g   Cholesterol 4mg   Sodium 150mg   **Exchanges:** 1 Starch,
1 Skim Milk

BREADS

Honey-Almond French Braid (page 72)

Cinnamon-Oatmeal Muffins

PREP: 8 MINUTES   COOK: 18 MINUTES

1½ cups all-purpose flour
 1 tablespoon baking powder
¼ teaspoon salt
¾ cup quick-cooking oats, uncooked
⅔ cup brown sugar
¾ teaspoon ground cinnamon
¾ cup skim milk
⅓ cup unsweetened applesauce
1½ tablespoons vegetable oil
 3 egg whites
    Vegetable cooking spray

Combine first 6 ingredients in a medium bowl; make a well in center of mixture. Combine milk, applesauce, oil, and egg white; add to dry ingredients, stirring just until dry ingredients are moistened.

Spoon batter into 12 muffin pan cups coated with cooking spray, filling each three-fourths full. Bake at 400° for 18 to 20 minutes or until golden. Remove from pan immediately. Yield: 1 dozen.

•**Per Muffin**: Calories 132   Carbohydrate 24.1g   Protein 3.8g   Fat 2.3g
Fiber 1.1g   Cholesterol 0mg   Sodium 98mg   **Exchanges**: 1½ Starch, ½ Fat

Cinnamon-Oatmeal Muffins

Applesauce Pancakes

PREP: 6 MINUTES   COOK: 10 MINUTES

   1 cup all-purpose flour
   1 teaspoon baking soda
 ⅛ teaspoon salt
   2 tablespoons toasted wheat germ
   1 cup nonfat buttermilk
 ¼ cup applesauce
   2 teaspoons vegetable oil
   1 egg, lightly beaten
      Vegetable cooking spray
      Reduced-calorie maple syrup (optional)
      Fresh fruit slices (optional)

   Combine first 4 ingredients in a medium bowl; make a well in center of mixture. Combine buttermilk and next 3 ingredients. Add buttermilk mixture to dry ingredients, stirring just until dry ingredients are moistened.

   Coat a nonstick griddle or nonstick skillet with cooking spray, and preheat to 350°. For each pancake, pour ¼ cup batter onto hot griddle, spreading to a 5-inch circle. Cook pancakes until tops are covered with bubbles and edges look cooked; turn pancakes, and cook other side. If desired, serve with maple syrup and fresh fruit slices. Yield: 10 (5-inch) pancakes.

•**Per Pancake:** Calories 81   Carbohydrate 12.8g   Protein 3.2g   Fat 1.8g
Fiber 0.6g   Cholesterol 23mg   Sodium 187mg   **Exchange:** 1 Starch

Applesauce Pancakes

Cinnamon French Toast

PREP: 3 MINUTES   COOK: 15 MINUTES

½ cup egg substitute
½ cup skim milk
½ to ¾ teaspoon ground cinnamon
    Vegetable cooking spray
1 tablespoon plus 1 teaspoon reduced-calorie margarine, divided
4 (1⅓-ounce) slices honey-wheatberry bread or
    whole wheat bread

Combine first 3 ingredients in a shallow bowl, stirring well with a wire whisk.

Coat a nonstick skillet with cooking spray. Add 1 teaspoon margarine; place over medium heat until margarine melts. Dip l bread slice into egg substitute mixture. Place coated bread in skillet; cook until browned and crisp on each side, turning once. Repeat with remaining margarine, bread, and egg substitute mixture. Yield: 4 servings.

•**Per Serving:** Calories 141   Carbohydrate 21.2g   Protein 7.1g   Fat 4.4g
Fiber 3.1g   Cholesterol 1mg   Sodium 248mg   **Exchanges:** 1½ Starch, 1 Fat

Rosemary Focaccia

PREP: 20 MINUTES   RISE: 1 HOUR   COOK: 20 MINUTES

  1 package active dry yeast
1¼ cups warm water (105° to 115°), divided
3¾ cups all-purpose flour, divided
  1 teaspoon salt, divided
  3 tablespoons margarine, melted
 ½ cup chopped fresh rosemary, divided
  2 tablespoons all-purpose flour
    Olive oil-flavored vegetable cooking spray
  4 cloves garlic, minced

Combine yeast and ¼ cup warm water; let stand 5 minutes. Combine yeast mixture, remaining 1 cup warm water, 2 cups flour, and ½ teaspoon salt in a large mixing bowl; beat at medium speed of an electric mixer until mixture is well blended. Cover and let rise in a warm place (85°), free from drafts, 1 hour or until doubled in bulk.

Punch dough down; stir in 1¾ cups flour, melted margarine, and ¼ cup rosemary.

Sprinkle 2 tablespoons flour evenly over work surface. Turn dough out onto floured surface, and knead until smooth and elastic (about 10 minutes). Divide dough in half. For each focaccia, roll or press 1 portion of dough into an 11-inch circle on a baking sheet coated with cooking spray. Poke holes in dough at 1-inch intervals with handle of a wooden spoon.

Coat top of each round with cooking spray; sprinkle evenly with remaining ¼ cup rosemary, remaining ½ teaspoon salt, and garlic. Bake at 400° for 20 minutes. Cut each circle into 12 squares or wedges. Yield: 24 servings.

•**Per serving:** Calories 89 Carbohydrate 15.8g Protein 2.3g Fat 1.7g
Fiber 0.6g Cholesterol 0mg Sodium 116mg **Exchange:** 1 Starch

Broccoli Cornbread

PREP: 10 MINUTES   COOK: 23 MINUTES

Vegetable cooking spray
1 tablespoon reduced-calorie margarine
½ (10-ounce) package frozen chopped broccoli, thawed and drained
1 (8½-ounce) package corn muffin mix
¾ cup 1% low-fat cottage cheese
½ cup egg substitute
½ cup finely chopped onion
1 (2-ounce) jar diced pimiento, drained
¼ teaspoon cracked pepper

Coat an 8-inch square pan with cooking spray. Add margarine, and place in a 425° oven for 3 minutes or until margarine melts.

Press broccoli between paper towels to remove excess moisture. Combine broccoli, muffin mix and remaining 5 ingredients, stirring well. Spoon into prepared pan. Bake at 425° for 23 minutes or until golden. Yield: 16 servings.

•**Per Serving**: Calories 82   Carbohydrate 12.2g   Protein 3.4g   Fat 2.2g
Fiber 0.9g   Cholesterol 0mg   Sodium 186mg   **Exchange**: 1 Starch

Broccoli Cornbread

Honey-Almond French Braid

PREP: 8 MiNUTES   COOK: 30 MINUTES

TECHNIQUE

Braid the 3 ropes of dough,
and pinch the loose ends
together to form 1 braided loaf.

1 (11-ounce) can refrigerated French bread dough
  Vegetable cooking spray
2 tablespoons honey
½ teaspoon water
⅛ teaspoon ground ginger
2 tablespoons sliced almonds

Unroll dough; cut into 3 equal pieces. Shape each portion into a rope. Place ropes on a baking sheet coated with cooking spray; (do not stretch). Braid ropes; pinch loose ends to seal. Combine honey, water, and ginger, stirring well. Brush braided dough with half of honey mixture.

Bake braid at 350° for 20 minutes. Remove from oven; brush with remaining honey mixture. Sprinkle with almonds. Bake 10 additional minutes or until loaf sounds hollow when tapped. Remove from baking sheet immediately. Serve warm. Yield: 10 servings. *(photo on page 63)*

•**Per Serving:** Calories 97   Carbohydrate 17.3g   Protein 3.3g   Fat 1.8g
Fiber 0.4g   Cholesterol 0mg   Sodium 195mg   **Exchange:** 1 Starch

Sesame-Garlic French Braid: Shape dough as directed above. Omit honey, water, ginger, and almonds. Cut 2 cloves of garlic into thin slices, and insert slices evenly into braid. Brush 1½ tablespoons melted reduced-calorie margarine over braid, and sprinkle with 2 teaspoons sesame seeds. Bake at 350° for 25 minutes or until loaf sounds hollow when tapped. Remove from baking sheet immediately. Serve warm. Yield: 10 servings.

DESSERTS

Frozen Lemon-Raspberry Pie
(page 83)

Apple Turnovers

PREP: 20 MINUTES   COOK: 15 MINUTES

TECHNIQUE

Cut the stacked sheets of phyllo into lengthwise strips. Use a ruler to help you cut straight strips.

Place 1 heaping tablespoon of filling at the base of each strip.

Fold the right bottom corner of the strip over the filling to form a triangle.

Fold the triangle back and forth to the end of the strip.

1 cup chopped reduced-calorie apple pie filling
¼ cup raisins
½ teaspoon apple pie spice
6 sheets frozen phyllo pastry, thawed
  Butter-flavored vegetable cooking spray
1 cup sifted powdered sugar
1 tablespoon plus 1 teaspoon low-fat milk

Combine first 3 ingredients in a small bowl; set aside.

Place 1 sheet of phyllo on a damp towel (keep remaining phyllo covered). Lightly coat phyllo with cooking spray. Place another sheet of phyllo over first sheet; coat with cooking spray. Cut stacked sheets lengthwise into 4 equal strips (each about 3¼ inches wide).

Working with one strip at a time, place 1 heaping tablespoon apple mixture at base of strip (keep remaining strips covered). Fold the right bottom corner over apple mixture to form a triangle. Continue folding the triangle back and forth to end of strip. Repeat folding process with next 3 strips. Place triangles, seam sides down, on a baking sheet coated with cooking spray. (Keep triangles covered before baking.) Repeat procedure twice with remaining phyllo sheets and apple mixture.

Bake at 400° for 15 minutes or until golden. Remove from baking sheet, and let cool 5 minutes on a wire rack. Combine powdered sugar and milk, stirring until smooth. Drizzle sugar mixture evenly over turnovers. Serve warm. Yield: 12 turnovers.

•**Per Turnover:** Calories 108   Carbohydrate 23.6g   Protein 1.2g   Fat 1.1g
Fiber 0.4g   Cholesterol 0mg   Sodium 72mg   **Exchanges:** 1 Starch, ½ Fruit

Pear-Cranberry Crumble

PREP: 10 MINUTES COOK: 40 MINUTES

 2 (16-ounce) cans pear halves in light syrup
½ cup dried cranberries
¼ cup plus 1 tablespoon all-purpose flour, divided
½ teaspoon ground allspice
    Vegetable cooking spray
⅔ cup quick-cooking oats, uncooked
¼ cup firmly packed brown sugar
¼ cup reduced-calorie stick margarine

Drain pears, reserving ¾ cup liquid. Discard remaining liquid.
Combine pears, ¾ cup liquid, and cranberries. Combine 1 table-
spoon flour and allspice; sprinkle over pear mixture, and toss lightly.
Spoon mixture into an 8-inch square pan coated with cooking spray.

Combine remaining ¼ cup flour, oats, and sugar. Cut in mar-
garine with a pastry blender until mixture resembles coarse meal.
Sprinkle oat mixture over pear mixture. Bake at 375° for 40 minutes.
Yield: 8 servings.

•**Per Serving:** Calories 170   Carbohydrate 33.3g   Protein 1.8g   Fat 4.3g
Fiber 3.6g   Cholesterol 0mg   Sodium 62mg   **Exchanges:** 1 Starch, 1 Fruit,
1 Fat

Tiramisù

½ cup plus 1 tablespoon Kahlúa or other coffee-flavored liqueur
¼ cup plus 1 tablespoon sugar, divided
2 tablespoons water
1 tablespoon plus 1 teaspoon instant espresso powder
¼ cup plus 2 tablespoons liquid fat-free hazelnut-flavored nondairy
   coffee creamer
1 cup light process cream cheese, softened
1½ cups frozen reduced-calorie whipped topping, thawed
1 (13.6-ounce) loaf fat-free pound cake, cut into 16 slices
  Unsweetened cocoa (optional)

Combine liqueur, 1 tablespoon sugar, water, and espresso powder, stirring until sugar and espresso powder dissolve. Spoon 2 tablespoons mixture into a medium bowl; set remaining mixture aside.

Add remaining ¼ cup sugar and creamer to 2 tablespoons liqueur mixture in bowl, stirring until sugar dissolves. Add cream cheese; beat at medium speed of an electric mixer until smooth. Fold in whipped topping.

Place 1 cake slice in each of 8 wine glasses or 8 (4-ounce) custard cups. Brush cake in glasses generously with half of reserved liqueur mixture. Spread cheese mixture evenly over cake. Top with remaining 8 cake slices. Gently press slices into glasses. Brush cake with remaining liqueur mixture. Sprinkle evenly with cocoa, if desired. Serve immediately. Yield: 8 servings.

•**Per Serving**: Calories 323 Carbohydrate 50.3g Protein 6.3g Fat 6.4g
Fiber 0.3g Cholesterol 16mg Sodium 924mg **Exchanges**: 3½ Starch, 1 Fat

Tiramisù

Irish Coffee-Caramel Dessert

PREP: 9 MINUTES   CHILL: 30 MINUTES

2 teaspoons unflavored gelatin
¼ cup cold water
1⅓ cups evaporated skimmed milk
2 tablespoons powdered sugar
¼ cup fat-free caramel-flavored syrup
¼ cup Irish cream liqueur
1 teaspoon instant coffee granules
¼ cup frozen reduced-calorie whipped topping, thawed

Sprinkle gelatin over cold water in a small saucepan; let stand 1 minute. Cook over low heat, stirring until gelatin dissolves, about 2 minutes. Stir in milk and next 4 ingredients.

Pour gelatin mixture evenly into 4 dessert dishes or parfait glasses. Cover and chill until set. Just before serving, top each serving with 1 tablespoon whipped topping. Yield: 4 servings.

•**Per Serving**: Calories 190   Carbohydrate 31.2g   Protein 8.5g   Fat 3.2g
Fiber 0.0g   Cholesterol 3mg   Sodium 153mg   **Exchanges**: 2 Starch, ½ Fat

Creamy Citrus Trifle

PREP: 20 MINUTES   CHILL: 3 HOURS

1 (3.4-ounce) package lemon instant pudding mix
2 cups fat-free milk
1 (8-ounce) carton low-fat sour cream
⅓ cup low-sugar orange marmalade
1 tablespoon dry sherry or unsweetened orange juice
8 ounces angel food cake, cut into ¾-inch cubes
2 (11-ounce) cans mandarin oranges in light syrup, drained

Combine pudding mix and milk, stirring until smooth. Stir in sour cream; set aside. Combine marmalade and sherry, stirring with a wire whisk until blended.

Arrange half of cake cubes in a 1½-quart trifle bowl or straight-sided glass bowl. Spoon half of pudding mixture over cake. Drizzle marmalade mixture over pudding mixture. Arrange half of oranges over marmalade mixture. Repeat layers with remaining cake, pudding mixture, and oranges. Cover and chill at least 3 hours. Yield: 8 servings.

•**Per Serving**: Calories 197   Carbohydrate 37.2g   Protein 4.7g   Fat 3.6g
Fiber 0.0g   Cholesterol 12mg   Sodium 341mg   **Exchanges**: 1½ Starch,
1 Fruit, 1 Fat

Rocky Road Ice Cream

PREP: 10 MINUTES   FREEZE: 10 MINUTES   STAND: 1 HOUR

1 (3.9-ounce) package chocolate instant pudding mix
2 tablespoons sugar
1 cup fat-free milk
1 (12-ounce) can evaporated skimmed milk
¾ cup miniature marshmallows
½ cup semisweet chocolate mini-morsels
¼ cup coarsely chopped unsalted dry roasted peanuts

Combine pudding mix and sugar in a large bowl. Gradually add fat-free milk and evaporated milk, stirring with a wire whisk until smooth. Stir in marshmallows, chocolate morsels, and peanuts.

Pour chocolate mixture into freezer can of a 2-quart hand-turned or electric freezer. Freeze according to manufacturer's instructions. Pack freezer with additional ice and rock salt, and let stand at least 1 hour before serving. Yield: 8 (½-cup) servings.

•**Per Serving:** Calories 203   Carbohydrate 33.2g   Protein 6.0g   Fat 6.2g
Fiber 1.0g   Cholesterol 2mg   Sodium 273mg   **Exchanges:** 1½ Starch,
½ Skim Milk, 1 Fat

Rocky Road Ice Cream

Strawberries 'n' Cream Pops

PREP: 10 MINUTES FREEZE: 2 HOURS

1 (8-ounce) carton plain nonfat yogurt
1 (8-ounce) package nonfat cream cheese
2 (10-ounce) packages frozen sweetened strawberries, thawed
8 (6-ounce) paper cups
8 wooden sticks

Place yogurt and cream cheese in container of an electric blender. Cover and process until smooth, stopping once to scrape down sides. Add strawberries, and process until smooth.

Spoon strawberry mixture evenly into paper cups. Cover tops of cups with aluminum foil, and insert a wooden stick through foil into center of each cup. Freeze until firm. To serve, remove aluminum foil; peel cup from pop. Yield: 8 servings.

•**Per Serving**: Calories 68 Carbohydrate 10.6g Protein 5.8g Fat 0.1g
Fiber 0.2g Cholesterol 6mg Sodium 192mg **Exchange**: 1 Fruit

For blueberry pops, substitute frozen blueberries for the strawberries.
Other fruits such as raspberries or peaches also offer a
change of taste for this three-ingredient recipe.

Frozen Lemon-Raspberry Pie

PREP: 15 MINUTES   FREEZE: 2 HOURS AND 15 MINUTES

1¾ cups reduced-fat gingersnap cookie crumbs (about 40 cookies)
  3 tablespoons reduced-calorie margarine, melted
  2 tablespoons minced crystallized ginger
  4 cups raspberry sorbet, softened
  4 cups lemon sorbet, softened
  3 cups fresh raspberries
  3 (1-ounce) squares white chocolate, melted
    Fresh mint sprigs (optional)

Combine first 3 ingredients, stirring well. Press into bottom of a 10-inch springform pan; freeze 15 minutes or until firm. Spread raspberry sorbet over crumb mixture. Freeze 1 hour. Spread lemon sorbet over raspberry sorbet. Cover and freeze 1 hour.

To serve, remove pie from pan. Arrange raspberries over lemon sorbet. Drizzle white chocolate over raspberries; slice pie into wedges. Garnish with mint sprigs, if desired. Yield: 12 servings.
(*photo on page 73*)

•**Per Serving**: Calories 312   Carbohydrate 58.4g   Protein 2.7g   Fat 7.8g
Fiber 2.7g   Cholesterol 8mg   Sodium 145mg   **Exchanges**: 2 Starch, 1 Fruit, 2 Fat

Banana Cream Pie

PREP: 11 MINUTES   COOK: 8 MINUTES   CHILL: 1½ HOURS

1 cup reduced-fat chocolate graham cracker crumbs
  (about 10 crackers)
¼ cup reduced-calorie margarine, melted
1 (3.4-ounce) package banana cream-flavored instant pudding mix
1 cup low-fat milk
¼ cup plus 1 tablespoon crème de cacao or other chocolate-
  flavored liqueur, divided
1¾ cups frozen reduced-calorie whipped topping, thawed and
  divided
1¼ cups peeled, sliced banana

Combine cracker crumbs and margarine, stirring well. Press into bottom and up sides of a 9-inch pieplate. Bake at 350° for 8 minutes. Remove from oven, and let cool on a wire rack.

Combine pudding mix, milk, and ¼ cup liqueur in a medium bowl, stirring with a wire whisk until smooth. Gently fold 1 cup whipped topping into pudding mixture.

Toss banana slices with remaining 1 tablespoon liqueur, and arrange over prepared crust. Spoon pudding mixture over banana slices. Cover and chill 1½ hours or until set. Pipe or spoon remaining ¾ cup whipped topping around edge of pie just before serving. Yield: 8 servings.

NOTE: For a nonalcoholic version: Omit crème de cacao. Increase milk to 1¼ cups to combine with pudding mix. Omit tossing bananas before placing in prepared crust.

•**Per Serving:** Calories 268   Carbohydrate 42.5g   Protein 3.3g   Fat 8.4g Fiber 1.1g   Cholesterol 1mg   Sodium 400mg   **Exchanges:** 2 Starch, 1 Fruit, 1 Fat

Sweet Potato Pie

PREP: 10 MINUTES   COOK: 1 HOUR AND 5 MINUTES

1 (14½-ounce) can no-sugar-added mashed sweet potatoes
2 tablespoons reduced-calorie margarine
¾ cup firmly packed brown sugar
1 teaspoon pumpkin pie spice
⅓ cup egg substitute
⅓ cup evaporated skimmed milk
1 (6-ounce) reduced-fat graham cracker pie crust

Place sweet potato and margarine in a medium-size microwave-safe bowl. Microwave at HIGH 3 minutes or until potato is thoroughly heated; stir well. Add brown sugar and pumpkin pie spice to potato mixture; stir well. Gradually add egg substitute and milk, stirring well. Pour potato mixture into pie crust.

Bake at 400° for 10 minutes. Reduce heat to 350°, and bake 55 additional minutes or until set. Let pie cool on a wire rack. Yield: 8 servings.

•**Per Serving:** Calories 261   Carbohydrate 50.1g   Protein 3.7g   Fat 5.0g
Fiber 2.1g   Cholesterol 0mg   Sodium 165mg   **Exchanges:** 3 Starch, 1 Fat

Malibu Brownie Torte

PREP: 15 MINUTES   COOK: 15 MINUTES   FREEZE: 2 HOURS

½ (20.5-ounce) package low-fat fudge brownie mix
⅓ cup water
    Vegetable cooking spray
 1 cup fat-free fudge topping, divided
 6 cups low-fat vanilla ice cream, softened
⅓ cup semisweet chocolate mini-morsels
¼ cup Malibu rum (or ¼ cup rum and ½ teaspoon coconut extract)
1½ tablespoons flaked coconut, toasted
    Strawberry fans (optional)

Combine ½ package brownie mix and ⅓ cup water, stirring just until dry ingredients are moistened. Reserve remaining brownie mix for another use. Pour batter into a 9-inch springform pan coated with cooking spray. Bake at 350° for 15 minutes or until edges pull away from pan slightly. Let cool in pan on a wire rack. Spread ½ cup fudge topping over brownie.

Combine ice cream, chocolate morsels, and rum in a large bowl, stirring well. Spread ice cream mixture over brownie. Freeze 2 hours or until firm.

To serve, remove torte from pan. Drizzle remaining ½ cup fudge topping over torte. Sprinkle with coconut. Garnish each slice with a strawberry fan, if desired. Yield: 16 servings.

•**Per Serving:** Calories 241   Carbohydrate 42.2g   Protein 4.2g   Fat 5.8g
Fiber 1.7g   Cholesterol 7mg   Sodium 158mg   **Exchanges:** 2½ Starch, 1 Fat

Malibu Brownie Torte

Chocolate Cream Cupcakes

Chocolate Cream Cupcakes

PREP: 15 MINUTES   COOK: 25 MINUTES

1 (20.5-ounce) package low-fat fudge brownie mix
⅔ cup water
   Vegetable cooking spray
½ (8-ounce) package Neufchâtel cheese
3 tablespoons sugar
1 teaspoon egg substitute
2 tablespoons semisweet chocolate morsels, melted

Combine brownie mix and water; stir until blended. Spoon into 12 muffin cups lined with paper liners coated with cooking spray.

Combine cheese and sugar, beating at medium speed of an electric mixer until light and fluffy. Add egg substitute, beating well. Stir in melted chocolate. Spoon 2 heaping teaspoons cheese mixture into center of each cupcake. Bake at 350° for 25 minutes or until centers are set. Remove from pan, and let cool on a wire rack. Yield: 1 dozen.

•**Per Cupcake**: Calories 256   Carbohydrate 44.9g   Protein 4.1g   Fat 6.7g
Fiber 1.5g   Cholesterol 7mg   Sodium 203mg   **Exchanges**: 3 Starch, 1 Fat

Pineapple Upside-Down Cake

Pineapple Upside-Down Cake

PREP: 15 MINUTES   COOK: 35 MINUTES

⅓ cup reduced-calorie margarine

¾ cup firmly packed brown sugar

⅓ cup chopped pecans

1 (15¼-ounce) can sliced pineapple in juice

½ (18.25-ounce) package reduced-fat yellow cake mix

¼ cup plus 2 tablespoons egg substitute

⅓ cup water

7 maraschino cherries with stems

Melt margarine in a 10-inch cast-iron skillet over low heat. Set aside 1 tablespoon margarine. Add sugar and pecans to margarine in skillet, stirring well. Drain pineapple, reserving ⅓ cup juice. Discard remaining juice. Arrange pineapple over sugar mixture.

Combine reserved 1 tablespoon margarine, ⅓ cup juice, cake mix, egg substitute, and water. Beat at low speed of an electric mixer 30 seconds. Beat at medium speed 2 minutes. Pour batter over pineapple in skillet. Bake at 350° for 35 minutes or until a wooden pick inserted in center comes out clean. Immediately invert cake onto a serving platter. Place cherries in centers of pineapple rings. Yield: 10 servings.

•**Per Serving:** Calories 254   Carbohydrate 44.5g   Protein 2.3g   Fat 8.0g   Fiber 0.7g   Cholesterol 0mg   Sodium 244mg   **Exchanges:** 2 Starch, 1 Fruit, 2 Fat

Individual Kahlúa Cheesecakes

PREP: 10 MINUTES   COOK: 20 MINUTES   CHILL: 1 HOUR

Vegetable cooking spray
6 chocolate wafer cookies, crushed
¾ cup Neufchâtel cheese, softened
¾ cup 1% low-fat cottage cheese
¼ cup plus 2 tablespoons sifted powdered sugar
½ cup egg substitute
¼ cup plus 2 tablespoons Kahlúa or other coffee-flavored liqueur
1½ teaspoons vanilla extract
3 tablespoons fat-free hot fudge topping, warmed

Coat 12 (2½-inch) paper baking cups with cooking spray; sprinkle chocolate wafer crumbs evenly on bottom and up sides of paper cups. Place paper cups in muffin pan cups.

Combine Neufchâtel cheese and next 5 ingredients in container of an electric blender; cover and process until mixture is smooth, stopping once to scrape down sides. Spoon cheese mixture evenly over wafer crumbs. Bake at 350° for 20 minutes or until almost set. Remove from oven; let cool to room temperature on a wire rack. Cover and chill.

To serve, remove paper liners, and place on serving plates. Drizzle evenly with hot fudge topping. Yield: 12 cheesecakes.

•**Per Cheesecake**: Calories 134   Carbohydrate 16.5g   Protein 4.9g   Fat 4.9g
Fiber 0.0g   Cholesterol 18mg   Sodium 171mg   **Exchanges**: 1 Starch, 1 Fat

Caramel-Oatmeal Bars

PREP: 8 MINUTES   COOK: 40 MINUTES   CHILL: 1 HOUR

1¼ cups quick-cooking oats, uncooked
1¼ cups all-purpose flour, divided
⅔ cup firmly packed brown sugar
½ cup reduced-calorie stick margarine
   Vegetable cooking spray
⅓ cup finely chopped walnuts
¾ cup fat-free caramel-flavored syrup

Combine oats, 1 cup flour, and sugar in a large bowl. Cut in margarine with a pastry blender until mixture resembles coarse meal. Press half of oat mixture into bottom of a 9-inch square pan coated with cooking spray. Bake at 350° for 15 minutes. Remove from oven; sprinkle walnuts over prepared crust.

Combine syrup and remaining ¼ cup flour; stir well. Pour syrup mixture over nuts. Sprinkle remaining oat mixture evenly over syrup mixture. Bake at 350° for 25 to 30 minutes or until golden. Let cool in pan on a wire rack. Cover and chill at least 1 hour. Cut into bars. Yield: 24 bars.

•**Per Bar**: Calories 116   Carbohydrate 19.0g   Protein 1.9g   Fat 3.6g
Fiber 0.7g   Cholesterol 0mg   Sodium 43mg   **Exchanges**: 1 Starch, 1 Fat

Cinnamon Sugar Cookies

PREP: **24** MINUTES   COOK: **6** MINUTES PER BATCH

  3 tablespoons reduced-calorie stick margarine, softened
 ⅔ cup plus 1½ tablespoons sugar, divided
  1 egg
1½ teaspoons vanilla extract
1½ cups plus 1½ teaspoons all-purpose flour, divided
 ½ teaspoon baking soda
 ½ teaspoon plus ⅛ teaspoon ground cinnamon, divided

Beat margarine at medium speed of an electric mixer until creamy; gradually add ⅔ cup sugar, beating well. Add egg and vanilla; beat well. Combine 1½ cups flour, baking soda, and ½ teaspoon cinnamon; gradually add to margarine mixture, beating well.

Sprinkle remaining 1½ teaspoons flour evenly over work surface. Turn dough out onto floured surface. Lightly flour hands, and shape dough into 26 balls. Combine remaining 1½ tablespoons sugar and remaining ⅛ teaspoon ground cinnamon. Roll balls in sugar mixture. Place balls, 3 inches apart, on ungreased cookie sheets. Pat each into a 2-inch circle. Bake at 375° for 6 to 8 minutes or until golden. Remove from cookie sheets; let cool completely on wire racks. Yield: 26 cookies.

•**Per Cookie**: Calories 60   Carbohydrate 11.4g   Protein 1.0g   Fat 1.1g
Fiber 0.2g   Cholesterol 8mg   Sodium 40mg   **Exchange**: 1 Starch

MEATLESS
MAIN
DISHES

Stuffed Poblanos (page 109)

Curried Vegetable Gratin

PREP: 15 MINUTES   COOK: 4 MINUTES

1 (16-ounce) package frozen carrots, cauliflower, and
    snow pea pods (or other frozen vegetable combination)
2 tablespoons all-purpose flour
1⅓ cups skim milk, divided
1 tablespoon reduced-calorie margarine
½ cup (2 ounces) shredded reduced-fat Swiss cheese
½ teaspoon curry powder
¼ teaspoon salt
   Vegetable cooking spray
2 tablespoons fine, dry breadcrumbs

Arrange frozen vegetables in a steamer basket over boiling water. Cover and steam 8 minutes or until crisp-tender; drain. Set aside, and keep warm.

Combine flour and ⅓ cup milk in a saucepan, stirring until smooth. Add remaining 1 cup milk and margarine; stir well. Cook over medium heat, stirring constantly, until milk mixture is thickened and bubbly. Remove from heat; add Swiss cheese, curry powder, and salt, stirring until cheese melts.

Spoon vegetables evenly into 4 (1½-cup) gratin or baking dishes coated with cooking spray. Spoon cheese mixture over vegetables. Sprinkle with breadcrumbs. Broil 5½ inches from heat (with electric oven door partially opened) 4 to 5 minutes or until lightly browned. Yield: 4 servings.

•**Per Serving**: Calories 153   Carbohydrate 17.3g   Protein 10.9g   Fat 4.8g   Fiber 2.8g   Cholesterol 10mg   Sodium 299mg   **Exchanges**: 1 Medium-Fat Meat, ½ Starch, 2 Vegetable

Vegetarian Egg Rolls

PREP: 15 MINUTES   COOK: 10 MINUTES

Vegetable cooking spray
5 cups finely preshredded cabbage
1 (14-ounce) can Chinese vegetables, drained
7 ounces soft tofu
1 tablespoon hoisin sauce
8 egg roll wrappers
2 teaspoons sesame oil, divided
½ cup Chinese sweet-and-sour sauce

Coat a large nonstick skillet with cooking spray; place over medium heat until hot. Add cabbage and Chinese vegetables; sauté 5 minutes or until cabbage is tender. Combine vegetable mixture, tofu, and hoisin sauce, stirring well.

Spoon vegetable mixture evenly into centers of egg roll wrappers. For each egg roll, fold one corner of wrapper over filling; then fold left and right corners of wrapper over filling. Push filling toward center of wrapper. Lightly brush exposed corner of wrapper with water. Tightly roll filled end of wrapper toward exposed corner; lightly press corner to seal securely.

Coat skillet with cooking spray; add 1 teaspoon sesame oil. Place over medium heat until hot. Add 4 egg rolls; cook 4 to 5 minutes or until golden, turning occasionally. Repeat procedure with remaining 1 teaspoon oil and 4 egg rolls. Serve with sweet-and-sour sauce. Yield: 4 servings (serving size: 2 egg rolls).

•**Per Serving**: Calories 307   Carbohydrate 58.5g   Protein 10.1g   Fat 3.9g Fiber 3.5g   Cholesterol 0mg   Sodium 540mg   **Exchanges**: 1 Lean Meat, 3 Starch, 2 Vegetable

TECHNIQUE

Spoon the vegetable mixture into the center of the wrapper, and fold one corner of the wrapper over the filling.

Fold the left and right corners of the wrapper over the filling, making an envelope. Brush the unfolded wrapper corner with water.

Roll the filled end toward the exposed corner, and press the corner to seal the package.

Portobello-Potato Pancake

PREP: 10 MINUTES   COOK: 30 MINUTES

1 (26-ounce) bag frozen shredded hash brown potatoes, thawed
1 small onion, thinly sliced
½ teaspoon salt
½ teaspoon freshly ground pepper
 Olive oil-flavored vegetable cooking spray
2 teaspoons olive oil, divided
6 ounces fresh portobello mushrooms, thinly sliced
1 (14-ounce) can artichoke hearts, drained and chopped
½ cup (2 ounces) freshly grated Asiago cheese, divided
2 tablespoons coarsely chopped walnuts
 Fresh rosemary sprigs (optional)

Combine first 4 ingredients in a large bowl, stirring well. Coat a 12-inch nonstick skillet with cooking spray. Add 1 teaspoon oil; place over medium heat until hot. Spoon potato mixture into skillet; press to smooth top. Cook 8 minutes or until potato is crisp and browned on bottom. Invert potato pancake onto a baking sheet.

Coat skillet with cooking spray; add remaining 1 teaspoon oil. Place over medium heat until hot. Return pancake to skillet, uncooked side down. Cook 8 minutes or until crisp and browned. Invert pancake onto baking sheet coated with cooking spray.

Coat skillet with cooking spray; place over medium-high heat until hot. Add mushrooms, and sauté 2 minutes or until tender. Remove from heat, and stir in artichoke.

Sprinkle pancake with ¼ cup cheese. Top with mushroom mixture. Sprinkle with walnuts; top with remaining ¼ cup cheese. Bake at 350° for 12 minutes or until thoroughly heated. Cut into 8 wedges. Garnish with rosemary sprigs, if desired. Yield: 4 servings (serving size: 2 wedges).

•**Per Serving**: Calories 296   Carbohydrate 43.7g   Protein 11.7g   Fat 9.5g
Fiber 2.8g   Cholesterol 10mg   Sodium 737mg   **Exchanges**: 1 High-Fat Meat,
2½ Starch, 1 Vegetable

Portobello-Potato Pancake

Vegetable-Cheese Pie

PREP: 10 MINUTES   COOK: 45 MINUTES

4½ cups frozen shredded hash brown potatoes, thawed
1 cup (4 ounces) shredded reduced-fat Cheddar cheese
¼ cup finely chopped green pepper
¼ cup chopped tomato
3 tablespoons finely chopped onion
¾ cup skim milk
¾ cup egg substitute
½ teaspoon salt
¼ teaspoon pepper
Vegetable cooking spray

Combine first 9 ingredients in a large bowl, stirring well. Pour mixture into a 9-inch pieplate coated with cooking spray. Bake, uncovered, at 350° for 45 minutes or until a knife inserted in center comes out clean. Let stand 10 minutes. Yield: 4 servings.

•**Per Serving:** Calories 201   Carbohydrate 21.3g   Protein 15.9g   Fat 5.7g
Fiber 0.9g   Cholesterol 19mg   Sodium 603mg   **Exchanges:** 2 Lean Meat,
1 Starch, 1 Vegetable

Store green peppers in the refrigerator in closed plastic bags.
The bags minimize moisture loss and prevent the pepper flavor from
being absorbed by other foods in the refrigerator.

Roasted Vegetable Pot Pie

PREP: 30 MINUTES   COOK: 30 MINUTES

2 (16-ounce) packages frozen stew vegetables, thawed
2 tablespoons fat-free Italian dressing
1 (25¾-ounce) jar fat-free chunky spaghetti sauce with
    mushrooms and sweet peppers
1 (15-ounce) can dark red kidney beans, drained
1 (10-ounce) can refrigerated pizza crust dough
1 teaspoon fennel seeds

Combine vegetables and Italian dressing, tossing well. Spoon vegetable mixture onto a large baking sheet. Bake at 450° for 20 minutes or until vegetables are lightly browned, stirring once. Remove from oven. Reduce oven temperature to 375°. Combine roasted vegetable mixture, spaghetti sauce, and kidney beans, stirring well. Spoon vegetable mixture into a 13- x 9- x 2-inch baking dish.

Unroll dough onto a work surface; sprinkle dough with fennel seeds. Roll dough to a 14- x 10-inch rectangle; place over vegetable mixture. Bake at 375° for 30 minutes or until lightly browned. Yield: 6 servings.

•**Per Serving**: Calories 297   Carbohydrate 57.9g   Protein 12.0g   Fat 1.9g   Fiber 5.1g   Cholesterol 0mg   Sodium 875mg   **Exchanges**: 1 Very Lean Meat, 3 Starch, 2 Vegetable

Spaghetti Squash
with White Bean Provençal

PREP: 20 MINUTES   COOK: 45 MINUTES

TECHNIQUE

Place squash on a cutting board, and cut squash in half lengthwise, using a large sharp knife.

Bake squash until tender, then scrape a fork along the inner surface to separate the squash into spaghetti-like strands.

1 (2½-pound) spaghetti squash
   Vegetable cooking spray
1 teaspoon roasted garlic-flavored vegetable oil
2 cups thinly sliced leek (about 1 leek)
2 (16-ounce) cans navy beans, drained
1 (14½-ounce) can no-salt-added stewed tomatoes, undrained
2 tablespoons chopped ripe olives
1 tablespoon balsamic vinegar
¼ teaspoon salt
¼ teaspoon pepper
   Fresh celery leaves (optional)

Wash squash; cut in half lengthwise. Remove and discard seeds. Place squash, cut sides down, in a 13- x 9- x 2-inch baking dish coated with cooking spray. Bake at 350° for 45 minutes or until tender; let cool slightly. Using a fork, remove spaghetti-like strands from squash; discard shells. Place strands on a platter; set aside, and keep warm.

Coat a saucepan with cooking spray; add oil. Place over medium-high heat until hot. Add leek; sauté 3 minutes or until tender. Add beans and tomatoes; cook over medium heat 5 minutes. Stir in olives and next 3 ingredients; cook until thoroughly heated. Spoon over squash. Garnish with celery leaves, if desired. Yield: 4 servings.

•**Per Serving:** Calories 226   Carbohydrate 43.0g   Protein 10.5g   Fat 2.9g
Fiber 6.8g   Cholesterol 0mg   Sodium 508mg   **Exchanges:** 1 Lean Meat,
1½ Starch, 2 Vegetable

Spaghetti Squash with White Bean Provençal

Italian Wonton Ravioli

PREP: 20 MINUTES   COOK: 15 MINUTES

*Make a star design by placing
1 wonton wrapper on top of
another.*

*Place the cheese mixture in the
center of the wonton star.*

*Moisten the edges of the wrap-
pers with water, and fold the
wrappers in half, bringing the
moistened edges together. Press
firmly.*

Olive-oil flavored vegetable cooking spray
1 cup chopped green pepper
2 cloves garlic, minced
2 cups fat-free chunky spaghetti sauce with mushrooms
   and sweet peppers
½ cup water
½ cup nonfat ricotta cheese
½ cup crumbled basil- and tomato-flavored feta cheese
   (or regular feta)
1½ tablespoons pesto
24 wonton wrappers
2 quarts water

Coat a large nonstick skillet with cooking spray; place over
medium-high heat until hot. Add chopped pepper and garlic; sauté
2 minutes. Add spaghetti sauce and ½ cup water. Bring mixture to a
boil; reduce heat, and simmer, uncovered, 10 minutes, stirring
occasionally. Set aside, and keep warm.

Combine cheeses and pesto in a small bowl. Place 1 wonton
wrapper on a work surface. Place a second wrapper (at a one-quarter
turn) on top of first wrapper, creating a star design. Place 1 tablespoon cheese mixture in center of star. Moisten edges of wrappers
with water; fold in half, bringing edges together. Press firmly. Repeat
procedure with remaining wrappers and cheese mixture.

Bring 2 quarts water to a boil in a large saucepan over high heat.
Add half of wontons; boil, uncovered, 1 minute. Remove from water,
using a slotted spoon; set aside, and keep warm. Repeat procedure
with remaining wontons. To serve, spoon one-fourth of spaghetti
sauce mixture onto each plate. Top each serving with 3 wontons.
Serve immediately. Yield: 4 servings.

•**Per Serving:** Calories 310   Carbohydrate 43.8g   Protein 15.5g   Fat 8.5g
Fiber 1.8g   Cholesterol 27mg   Sodium 990mg   **Exchanges:** 1 Medium-Fat
Meat, 2 Starch, 2 Vegetable

Spinach Lasagna

PREP: 20 MINUTES   COOK: 30 MINUTES

2 cups 1% low-fat cottage cheese
½ cup egg substitute
2 (10-ounce) packages frozen chopped spinach, thawed and
   drained well
1 (25¾-ounce) jar fat-free spaghetti sauce with mushrooms
9 cooked lasagna noodles (cooked without salt or fat)
2 cups (8 ounces) shredded part-skim mozzarella cheese
¼ cup plus 2 tablespoons grated Parmesan cheese

Combine first 3 ingredients in a medium bowl; stir well, and set aside.

Spread ½ cup spaghetti sauce in a 13- x 9- x 2-inch baking dish. Place 3 noodles over sauce; spoon one-third of spinach mixture over noodles. Top with one-third of remaining spaghetti sauce, ½ cup mozzarella cheese, and 2 tablespoons Parmesan cheese. Repeat procedure twice with remaining noodles, spinach mixture, spaghetti sauce, 1 cup mozzarella, and remaining Parmesan cheese. Top with remaining ½ cup mozzarella cheese. Bake, uncovered, at 350° for 30 to 35 minutes or until thoroughly heated. Let stand 10 minutes. Yield: 8 servings.

•**Per Serving**: Calories 278   Carbohydrate 30.2g   Protein 23.6g   Fat 6.9g   Fiber 3.6g   Cholesterol 22mg   Sodium 803mg   **Exchanges**: 3 Lean Meat, 1 Starch, 3 Vegetable

Black Bean Lasagna Rolls

PREP: 28 MINUTES   COOK: 25 MINUTES

1 cup (4 ounces) shredded reduced-fat Monterey Jack cheese
1 (15-ounce) carton part-skim ricotta cheese
1 (4½-ounce) can chopped green chiles, drained
½ teaspoon chili powder
⅛ teaspoon salt
8 lasagna noodles, uncooked
2 cups canned drained no-salt-added black beans
   Vegetable cooking spray
1 (15½-ounce) jar no-salt-added salsa
   Fresh cilantro sprigs (optional)

Combine first 5 ingredients, stirring well.

Cook lasagna noodles according to package directions, omitting salt and fat; drain well.

Spread cheese mixture over one side of each noodle. Spoon black beans evenly over cheese mixture. Roll up noodles, jellyroll fashion, beginning at narrow ends.

Place lasagna rolls, seam sides down, in an 11- x 7- x 1½-inch baking dish coated with cooking spray. Pour salsa over rolls. Cover and bake at 350° for 25 minutes or until thoroughly heated. Garnish with cilantro sprigs, if desired. Yield: 8 servings.

•**Per Serving:** Calories 295   Carbohydrate 37.8g   Protein 18.8g   Fat 7.8g
Fiber 2.8g   Cholesterol 26mg   Sodium 387mg   **Exchanges:** 2 Lean Meat,
2 Starch, 1 Vegetable

Black Bean Lasagna Rolls

Pasta with Peanut Sauce

PREP: 16 MINUTES   COOK: 4 MINUTES

    8 ounces spaghetti, uncooked
    3 medium-size yellow squash
    1 medium-size sweet red pepper
    6 green onions, cut into 2-inch pieces
    1 tablespoon dark sesame oil
    1 tablespoon minced garlic
  ¼ cup reduced-fat creamy peanut spread
  ¼ cup low-sodium soy sauce
    3 tablespoons fresh lime juice
    1 tablespoon sugar
    1 teaspoon dried crushed red pepper

Cook spaghetti according to package directions, omitting salt and fat. Drain.

Meanwhile, cut squash in half lengthwise; cut halves into slices. Seed sweet red pepper, and cut into thin strips. Cook squash, sweet red pepper, and green onions in a saucepan in boiling water to cover 1 to 2 minutes or until crisp-tender. Drain vegetables.

Heat oil in a large nonstick skillet over medium heat until hot. Add garlic; cook, stirring constantly, 1 minute. Add peanut spread, stirring until smooth. Stir in soy sauce and remaining 3 ingredients.

Add vegetable mixture to skillet, tossing gently to coat. Remove vegetable mixture from skillet with a slotted spoon. Add cooked spaghetti to sauce in skillet, tossing to coat. Transfer spaghetti to a serving plate, and top with vegetable mixture. Serve immediately. Yield: 5 (1-cup) servings.

•**Per serving:** Calories 339   Carbohydrate 50.3g   Protein 11.2g   Fat 11.3g Fiber 4.0g   Cholesterol 0mg   Sodium 497mg   **Exchanges:** 1 Medium-Fat Meat, 3 Starch, 1 Fat

Stuffed Poblanos

PREP: 40 MINUTES   COOK: 20 MINUTES

10 large poblano peppers
 1 (7½-ounce) package pinto beans and rice mix
 1 cup frozen whole-kernel corn, thawed
 1 cup (4 ounces) shredded reduced-fat Monterey Jack cheese
 1 tablespoon taco seasoning mix
 1 (15-ounce) can no-salt-added crushed tomatoes, undrained
 1 (15½-ounce) jar no-salt-added mild salsa

TECHNIQUE

Cut a strip from the long side
of each pepper.

Chop enough of the pepper
strips to get ½ cup chopped
pepper.

Cut a lengthwise strip from each pepper. Remove and discard seeds from peppers. Chop enough of pepper strips to measure ½ cup; reserve remaining strips for another use. Cook peppers in boiling water to cover 5 minutes; drain and set aside.

Cook bean mix according to package directions, omitting fat and seasoning packet. Combine chopped pepper, bean mix, corn, and next 3 ingredients. Spoon evenly into peppers; place peppers in a 13- x 9- x 2-inch baking dish. Add hot water to dish to a depth of ¼ inch. Bake at 350° for 20 minutes or until thoroughly heated.

Position knife blade in food processor bowl; add salsa. Process until smooth. Spoon salsa onto plates; top with peppers. Yield: 5 servings (serving size: 2 stuffed peppers plus salsa). (*photo on page 95*)

•**Per Serving:** Calories 335 Carbohydrate 56.8g Protein 17.2g Fat 5.3g
Fiber 6.0g Cholesterol 15mg Sodium 548mg **Exchanges:** 1 Lean Meat,
3 Starch, 2 Vegetable

Risotto with Peas and Peppers

PREP: 15 MINUTES   COOK: 30 MINUTES

  1 (14½-ounce) can vegetable broth
2¾ cups water
     Vegetable cooking spray
  1 cup plus 2 tablespoons Arborio rice, uncooked
 ¼ cup diced dried tomato (packed without oil)
 ⅔ cup frozen English peas, thawed
 ⅔ cup freshly grated Parmesan cheese
 ⅓ cup commercial roasted red pepper, drained and chopped
  1 teaspoon dried Italian seasoning
 ½ teaspoon pepper

Combine broth and water in a medium saucepan; place over medium heat. Cover and bring to a simmer; reduce heat to low, and keep warm. (Do not boil.)

Coat a large saucepan with cooking spray; place over medium-low heat until hot. Add rice and 1 cup simmering broth mixture. Cook, stirring constantly, until most of liquid is absorbed. Add 1½ cups broth mixture, ½ cup at a time, cooking and stirring constantly until each ½ cup addition is absorbed. Stir in tomato. Add remaining 2 cups broth mixture, ½ cup at a time, cooking and stirring constantly until each ½ cup addition is absorbed. (Rice will be tender and will have a creamy consistency.) Add peas and remaining ingredients, stirring until cheese melts; serve immediately. Yield: 4 (1-cup) servings.

•**Per Serving**: Calories 303   Carbohydrate 54.0g   Protein 10.6g   Fat 4.7g   Fiber 3.0g   Cholesterol 9mg   Sodium 857mg   **Exchanges**: 1 Medium-Fat Meat, 3½ Starch

Vegetable Strata

PREP: 12 MINUTES   CHILL: 8 HOURS   COOK: 40 MINUTES

¾ cup chopped fresh broccoli
2 (1-ounce) slices white bread, cubed
  Butter-flavored vegetable cooking spray
½ cup (2 ounces) shredded reduced-fat Jarlsberg cheese
2 tablespoons coarsely shredded carrot
1 tablespoon chopped sweet red pepper
1 tablespoon chopped green onions
¾ cup low-fat milk
½ cup egg substitute
¼ teaspoon dry mustard
¼ teaspoon hot sauce
¼ teaspoon low-sodium Worcestershire sauce
⅛ teaspoon pepper
  Dash of salt

Arrange broccoli in a vegetable steamer over boiling water. Cover and steam 3 minutes or until crisp-tender. Set aside.

Place bread cubes in a 1-quart casserole coated with cooking spray; sprinkle with cheese. Top with broccoli, carrot, red pepper, and green onions. Combine milk and remaining ingredients in a small bowl, stirring well; pour over broccoli mixture. Cover and chill 8 hours.

Remove from refrigerator, and let stand, covered, at room temperature 30 minutes. Bake, uncovered, at 350° for 40 minutes or until set. Let stand 10 minutes before serving. Yield: 2 servings.

•**Per Serving:** Calories 262 Carbohydrate 26.0g   Protein 23.1g   Fat 7.5g Fiber 3.2g   Cholesterol 22mg Sodium 428mg   **Exchanges**: 2 Medium-Fat Meat, 1 Starch, 2 Vegetable

Spinach and Mushroom Omelet

PREP: 16 MINUTES   COOK: 8 MINUTES

Butter-flavored vegetable cooking spray
1 cup sliced fresh mushrooms
1 tablespoon chopped green onions
3 cups loosely packed fresh spinach, coarsely chopped
2 tablespoons light process cream cheese product, softened
½ cup egg substitute
⅛ teaspoon salt
⅛ teaspoon pepper
1 egg
2 tablespoons (½ ounce) shredded reduced-fat sharp
   Cheddar cheese
2 teaspoons chopped fresh flat-leaf parsley

Coat a 10-inch nonstick skillet with cooking spray; place over medium-high heat until hot. Add mushrooms and green onions; sauté until tender. Remove from skillet. Set aside, and keep warm.

Add spinach to skillet; sauté until spinach wilts. Remove from heat; stir in cream cheese. Remove from skillet, and keep warm.

Wipe skillet with a paper towel. Combine egg substitute and next 3 ingredients in a small bowl, stirring well.

Coat skillet with cooking spray; place over medium heat until hot. Pour egg substitute mixture into skillet. As mixture begins to cook, gently lift edges of omelet with a spatula, and tilt pan to allow uncooked portion to flow underneath. When set, spoon mushroom mixture, spinach mixture, and Cheddar cheese over half of omelet. Loosen omelet with a spatula, and carefully fold in half. Cook an additional 1 to 2 minutes or until cheese begins to melt. Slide omelet onto a serving plate; cut in half. Sprinkle with parsley. Yield: 2 servings.

•**Per Serving:** Calories 145   Carbohydrate 6.2g   Protein 15.0g   Fat 7.0g
Fiber 3.2g   Cholesterol 123mg   Sodium 440mg   **Exchanges:** 2 Lean Meat,
1 Vegetable

MEATS, POULTRY & SEAFOOD

Italian Chicken Rolls (page 128)

Simple Beef Stroganoff

PREP: 10 MINUTES   COOK: 12 MINUTES

¾ pound lean boneless top sirloin steak
  Vegetable cooking spray
½ cup sliced onion
 1 pound fresh mushrooms, sliced
¼ cup dry white wine
¼ teaspoon salt
¼ teaspoon freshly ground pepper
 1 (10¾-ounce) can reduced-fat, reduced-sodium cream
    of mushroom soup
½ cup nonfat sour cream
4½ cups cooked egg noodles (cooked without salt or fat)

Trim fat from steak; cut steak into thin slices. Coat a nonstick skillet with cooking spray; place over medium-high heat until hot. Add steak; sauté 5 minutes. Add onion and mushrooms; sauté 5 minutes. Reduce heat to medium-low.

Add wine, salt, and pepper; cook 2 minutes. Combine soup and sour cream; stir into steak mixture. Cook until thoroughly heated. Serve over noodles. Yield: 6 servings.

•**Per Serving**: Calories 307   Carbohydrate 40.2g   Protein 21.7g   Fat 6.3g Fiber 4.1g   Cholesterol 78mg   Sodium 357mg   **Exchanges**: 2 Lean Meat, 2 Starch, 2 Vegetable

Smothered Steak

PREP: 10 MINUTES   COOK: 8 HOURS

1 (1½-pound) lean boneless round tip steak
3 tablespoons all-purpose flour
¼ teaspoon pepper
1 (14½-ounce) can no-salt-added stewed tomatoes, undrained
1 (10-ounce) package frozen chopped onion, celery, and pepper
    blend, thawed
3 tablespoons low-sodium Worcestershire sauce
1 tablespoon red wine vinegar
¼ teaspoon salt
3 cups cooked long-grain rice (cooked without salt or fat)

Trim fat from steak; cut steak into 1½-inch pieces. Place steak in a 4-quart electric slow cooker. Add flour and pepper; toss. Add tomatoes and next 4 ingredients; stir well.

Cover and cook on low setting 8 hours or until steak is tender, stirring once. Spoon over rice. Yield: 6 servings.

•**Per Serving:** Calories 312   Carbohydrate 36.5g   Protein 27.9g   Fat 5.1g
Fiber 0.6g   Cholesterol 68mg   Sodium 225mg   **Exchanges:** 3 Lean Meat,
1½ Starch, 1 Vegetable

*No watching, no stirring, and no turning. Just put the
ingredients into a slow cooker, and forget about it for awhile.
Dinner will simmer as you go about your day.*

Glazed Sirloin with Leeks

PREP: 10 MINUTES   COOK: 10 MINUTES

- 2 (1-pound) lean boneless top sirloin steaks (½ inch thick)
- ½ teaspoon salt
- ¼ teaspoon pepper
- 8 medium leeks
- ½ cup no-sugar-added peach spread
- ¼ cup plus 2 tablespoons honey mustard
- 1 tablespoon fresh lime juice
- 2 teaspoons olive oil
- ¼ teaspoon ground coriander
   Vegetable cooking spray
   Fresh cilantro leaves (optional)
   Fresh lime and peach slices (optional)

Sprinkle steaks with salt and pepper; set aside. Remove and discard roots, tough outer leaves, and tops from leeks, leaving 2 inches of dark leaves. Set aside.

Combine peach spread and next 4 ingredients in a glass measure. Microwave at HIGH 1 minute; set aside half of mixture.

Coat grill rack with cooking spray; place on grill over medium coals (300° to 350°) Place steaks and leeks on rack; grill, covered, 5 minutes on each side or until steaks are desired degree of doneness, basting often with half of peach mixture. Serve with reserved peach mixture. If desired, garnish with cilantro and lime and peach slices. Yield: 8 servings.

•**Per Serving**: Calories 294   Carbohydrate 28.0g   Protein 27.2g   Fat 7.6g
Fiber 1.1g   Cholesterol 76mg   Sodium 262mg   **Exchanges**: 3 Lean Meat,
2 Vegetable, 1 Fruit

Glazed Sirloin with Leeks

Gourmet Grilled Pizzas

PREP: 15 MINUTES   COOK: 13 MINUTES

TECHNIQUE

Cut the tenderloin lengthwise down the center, but don't cut all the way through, so that one long side will be connected.

1 small fennel bulb (about ½ pound)
1 (¾-pound) beef tenderloin
¼ teaspoon salt
¼ teaspoon freshly ground pepper
  Vegetable cooking spray
1 (6-ounce) package sliced fresh portobello mushrooms
4 (6-inch) focaccia rounds
½ cup tomato chutney
2 ounces thinly sliced fontina cheese

Trim tough outer stalks from fennel. Cut bulb in half lengthwise; remove and discard core. Set bulb aside.

Cut tenderloin lengthwise down center, cutting to, but not through, bottom. Flip cut piece out to enlarge tenderloin, and sprinkle with salt and pepper.

Coat grill rack with cooking spray; place on grill over medium-hot coals (350° to 400°). Place tenderloin and fennel on rack; grill, covered, 5 minutes. Add mushrooms. Grill 5 additional minutes or until tenderloin is desired degree of doneness and vegetables are tender, turning tenderloin and vegetables once. Cut tenderloin and fennel into thin slices.

Arrange tenderloin, fennel, and mushrooms evenly over focaccia rounds. Spoon 2 tablespoons chutney over each round; top with cheese. Return to grill rack; grill 3 minutes or until cheese melts. Yield: 4 servings.

•**Per Serving**: Calories 363   Carbohydrate 28.7g   Protein 31.9g   Fat 13.7g
Fiber 2.3g   Cholesterol 88mg   Sodium 357mg   **Exchanges**: 3 Medium-Fat
Meat, 1 Starch, 1 Vegetable

Gourmet Grilled Pizzas

Veal Chops with Wild Mushrooms

PREP: 18 MINUTES   COOK: 30 MINUTES

      Vegetable cooking spray
  4 (6-ounce) lean veal loin chops (¾ inch thick)
  ½ cup fresh shiitake mushrooms, thinly sliced
  ½ cup fresh oyster mushrooms, thinly sliced
  1 cup canned no-salt-added chicken broth, undiluted
  ½ cup evaporated skimmed milk
  ¼ cup (1 ounce) shredded reduced-fat Swiss cheese
  1 teaspoon minced fresh thyme

   Coat a large nonstick skillet with cooking spray; place over medium heat until hot. Add veal chops; cook 2 to 3 minutes on each side or until browned. Remove chops from skillet. Drain and pat dry with paper towels. Set chops aside. Wipe drippings from skillet with a paper towel.

   Coat skillet with cooking spray; place over medium-high heat until hot. Add mushrooms; sauté until tender. Remove mushrooms from skillet; set aside.

   Return chops to skillet; pour broth over chops. Bring to a boil; cover, reduce heat, and simmer 20 to 25 minutes or until chops are tender. Remove chops from skillet; set aside, and keep warm.

   Add milk to liquid in skillet. Bring to a boil; cook, stirring constantly, 1 minute or until thickened. Stir in mushrooms, cheese, and thyme. Cook, stirring constantly, until cheese melts. Spoon sauce evenly over chops. Serve immediately. Yield: 4 servings.

•**Per Serving**: Calories 199   Carbohydrate 6.2g   Protein 28.6g   Fat 6.0g
Fiber 0.4g   Cholesterol 96mg   Sodium 186mg   **Exchanges**: 3 Lean Meat, 1 Vegetable

Moussaka

PREP: 45 MINUTES   COOK: 25 MINUTES

2 small eggplants (about ¾ pound each)
   Olive-oil flavored vegetable cooking spray
1 pound lean ground lamb (or ground round)
1 (27½-ounce) jar fat-free chunky spaghetti sauce
      with mushrooms
1 teaspoon ground cinnamon
½ teaspoon pepper
1 (10¾-ounce) can reduced-fat, reduced-sodium cream of
      mushroom soup
⅓ cup water
2 tablespoons fine, dry breadcrumbs
2 tablespoons freshly grated Parmesan cheese

Peel eggplants, and cut crosswise into ¼-inch-thick slices. Place on a large baking sheet coated with cooking spray. Coat slices with cooking spray. Bake at 375° for 25 minutes or until eggplant is tender and lightly browned, turning once. Let cool slightly.

Coat a large nonstick skillet with cooking spray; place over medium-high heat until hot. Add meat, and cook until browned, stirring until it crumbles. Drain and pat dry with paper towels. Wipe drippings from skillet with a paper towel.

Return meat to skillet; add spaghetti sauce, cinnamon, and pepper. Bring to a boil; reduce heat, and simmer, uncovered, 5 minutes or until meat mixture is thickened, stirring occasionally.

Coat an 11- x 7- x 1½-inch baking dish with cooking spray. Arrange half of eggplant in dish; top with half of meat mixture. Repeat layers with remaining eggplant and remaining meat mixture. Combine soup and water in a bowl, stirring until smooth; pour over meat mixture. Combine breadcrumbs and cheese; sprinkle over soup mixture. Bake, uncovered, at 375° for 25 minutes or until browned and bubbly. Yield: 6 servings.

•Per Serving: Calories 248   Carbohydrate 23.3g   Protein 22.9g   Fat 7.8g
Fiber 4.2g   Cholesterol 59mg   Sodium 685mg   Exchanges: 3 Lean Meat,
4 Vegetable

Quick Pork Parmesan

PREP: 10 MINUTES   COOK: 30 MINUTES

4 (4-ounce) boneless center-cut pork loin chops
⅓ cup fine, dry breadcrumbs
2 tablespoons grated Parmesan cheese
¼ cup egg substitute
  Vegetable cooking spray
1½ cups low-fat spaghetti sauce with garlic and herbs
½ cup (2 ounces) shredded reduced-fat mozzarella cheese

Trim fat from pork chops. Place chops between two sheets of heavy-duty plastic wrap, and flatten to ¼-inch thickness, using a meat mallet or rolling pin.

Combine breadcrumbs and Parmesan cheese in a small bowl. Dip chops in egg substitute; dredge in breadcrumb mixture.

Coat a large nonstick skillet with cooking spray; place over medium heat until hot. Add chops, and cook 1 to 2 minutes on each side or until browned. Arrange chops in an 8-inch square baking dish coated with cooking spray. Pour spaghetti sauce over chops. Cover and bake at 350° for 25 minutes or until chops are tender. Uncover; sprinkle with mozzarella cheese. Bake 5 additional minutes or until cheese melts. Serve immediately. Yield: 4 servings.

•**Per Serving:** Calories 322   Carbohydrate 17.1g   Protein 34.6g   Fat 11.8g
Fiber 2.0g   Cholesterol 79mg   Sodium 614mg   **Exchanges:** 4 Lean Meat,
½ Starch, 2 Vegetable

Braised Pork Marsala

PREP: 5 MINUTES   COOK: 10 MINUTES

    1 (1-pound) pork tenderloin
    ¼ cup all-purpose flour
    ⅛ teaspoon salt
    1 tablespoon margarine
    ¾ cup Marsala wine
    1 teaspoon beef-flavored bouillon granules
    ¼ teaspoon freshly ground pepper
    2 cups cooked capellini (cooked without salt or fat)

Trim fat from tenderloin; cut tenderloin into ½-inch-thick slices. Combine flour and salt in a heavy-duty, zip-top plastic bag. Seal bag; shake well. Add tenderloin. Seal bag; shake until well coated.

Melt margarine in a nonstick skillet over medium heat. Add tenderloin; cook until browned, turning once. Remove from skillet. Add wine, bouillon granules, and pepper to skillet; bring to a boil. Reduce heat, and simmer, uncovered, 2 minutes. Return tenderloin to skillet; cover and simmer 2 minutes or until sauce is thickened. Serve over pasta. Yield: 4 servings.

•**Per Serving**: Calories 340   Carbohydrate 37.6g   Protein 29.7g   Fat 6.6g
Fiber 1.9g   Cholesterol 74mg   Sodium 403mg   **Exchanges**: 3 Lean Meat,
2½ Starch

Tenderloins with Cream Sauce

PREP: 12 MINUTES   COOK: 25 MINUTES

 Vegetable cooking spray
2 (¾-pound) pork tenderloins
¾ cup low-fat milk
1½ tablespoons all-purpose flour, divided
3 tablespoons Dijon mustard
2 tablespoons dry white wine
¼ cup nonfat sour cream
⅛ teaspoon pepper
 Fresh rosemary sprigs (optional)

Coat grill rack with cooking spray; place on grill over medium-hot coals (350° to 400°). Insert meat thermometer into thickest part of one tenderloin, if desired. Place tenderloins on rack. Grill, covered, 25 to 30 minutes or until meat thermometer registers 160°, turning occasionally.

Combine milk and 1 tablespoon flour in a saucepan, stirring until smooth. Cook over medium heat, stirring constantly, until thickened. Stir in mustard and wine; remove from heat. Combine remaining 1½ teaspoons flour and sour cream; add to milk mixture, stirring well. Stir in pepper. Serve with tenderloins. Garnish with rosemary, if desired. Yield: 6 servings.

•**Per Serving:** Calories 188   Carbohydrate 4.3g   Protein 28.1g   Fat 5.3g
Fiber 0.1g   Cholesterol 86mg   Sodium 307mg   **Exchanges:** 3 Lean Meat

Tenderloins with Cream Sauce

Orange-Glazed Ham with Sweet Potatoes

PREP: 7 MINUTES   COOK: 1 HOUR AND 30 MINUTES

  1 (2-pound) low-fat boneless cooked honey ham
     Vegetable cooking spray
¾ cup low-sugar orange marmalade
  3 tablespoons brown sugar
  1 tablespoon honey mustard
¼ teaspoon ground ginger
  1 (15¼-ounce) can unsweetened pineapple chunks in juice
  2 (15-ounce) cans sweet potatoes in light syrup, drained

Place ham in a shallow roasting pan coated with cooking spray. Cover and bake at 325° for 1 hour.

Combine marmalade and next 3 ingredients. Uncover ham, and brush with ⅓ cup marmalade mixture. Reserve remaining marmalade mixture.

Drain pineapple chunks, reserving ¼ cup juice. Reserve remaining juice for another use. Combine pineapple and sweet potatoes. Add ¼ cup pineapple juice to reserved marmalade mixture. Pour marmalade mixture over sweet potatoes and pineapple; toss lightly. Arrange sweet potato mixture around ham. Bake, uncovered, 30 additional minutes or until ham and potato are thoroughly heated. Yield: 10 servings.

•**Per Serving**: Calories 205   Carbohydrate 27.9g   Protein 16.3g   Fat 2.8g   Fiber 1.5g   Cholesterol 40mg   Sodium 663mg   **Exchanges**: 2 Very Lean Meat, 1 Starch, 1 Fruit

Salsa Chicken

PREP: 30 MINUTES   COOK: 10 MINUTES

6 (6-inch) corn tortillas
   Vegetable cooking spray
2 cups chopped cooked chicken breast (skinned before
   cooking and cooked without salt)
½ cup fat-free roasted garlic-flavored salsa
   (or regular salsa), divided
2 cups chopped onion
1 (4½-ounce) can chopped green chiles, undrained
1 cup (4 ounces) shredded reduced-fat Monterey Jack cheese
½ cup nonfat sour cream, divided

TECHNIQUE

Stack 3 tortillas, and use kitchen scissors to cut them into strips about ½ inch wide.

Cut tortillas into ½-inch-wide strips. Place strips in a single layer on an ungreased baking sheet, and coat strips with cooking spray. Bake at 350° for 10 minutes or until crisp. Let cool.

Combine chicken and ¼ cup salsa in a large nonstick skillet. Bring to a boil over high heat. Reduce heat to medium-high, and cook 2 minutes, stirring occasionally. Remove from skillet. Set aside, and keep warm. Wipe skillet dry with paper towels.

Coat skillet with cooking spray; place over medium-high heat until hot. Add onion; sauté 2 minutes. Add green chiles, and sauté 2 minutes. Add cheese and ¼ cup sour cream; stir until cheese melts.

To serve, arrange tortilla strips evenly on individual serving plates. Top tortilla strips evenly with chicken mixture. Spoon onion mixture evenly over chicken mixture. Top each serving with 1 tablespoon of remaining salsa and 1 tablespoon of remaining sour cream. Yield: 4 servings.

•**Per Serving:** Calories 333   Carbohydrate 25.7g   Protein 35.1g   Fat 9.2g Fiber 3.2g   Cholesterol 79mg   Sodium 531mg   **Exchanges:** 4 Lean Meat, 1½ Starch, 1 Vegetable

Italian Chicken Rolls

PREP: 15 MINUTES   COOK: 35 MINUTES

    6 (4-ounce) skinned, boned chicken breast halves
 ¼ teaspoon salt
 ¼ teaspoon pepper
 ½ cup chopped commercial roasted red pepper
 ⅓ cup light process cream cheese, softened
 ¼ cup pesto
 ¾ cup crushed corn flakes cereal
    3 tablespoons chopped fresh parsley
 ½ teaspoon paprika
      Vegetable cooking spray
      Fresh thyme sprigs (optional)

Place chicken between 2 sheets of heavy-duty plastic wrap; flatten to ¼-inch thickness, using a meat mallet or rolling pin. Sprinkle with salt and ¼ teaspoon pepper; set aside.

Combine red pepper, cream cheese, and pesto in a small bowl, stirring until smooth. Spread cheese mixture evenly over chicken breasts. Roll up, jellyroll fashion; secure with wooden picks.

Combine crushed cereal, parsley, and paprika. Dredge chicken in cereal mixture. Place in an 11- x 7- x 1½-inch baking dish coated with cooking spray. Bake, uncovered, at 350° for 35 minutes; let stand 10 minutes. Remove wooden picks from chicken, and slice each roll into 6 rounds. Garnish with thyme sprigs, if desired. Yield: 6 servings. *(photo on page 113)*

•**Per Serving**: Calories 253   Carbohydrate 12.1g   Protein 29.7g   Fat 9.0g
Fiber 0.7g   Cholesterol 75mg   Sodium 506mg   **Exchanges:** 3 Lean Meat,
1 Starch

Crispy Cheese-Filled Chicken

PREP: 19 MINUTES   COOK: 1 HOUR

4 (6-ounce) skinned chicken breast halves
3 ounces reduced-fat extra-sharp Cheddar cheese
1 tablespoon Dijon mustard
1 cup crushed corn flakes cereal
1 teaspoon salt-free spicy pepper seasoning
1 teaspoon dried parsley flakes
½ cup nonfat buttermilk
   Vegetable cooking spray

Cut a 2-inch-long slit in the meaty side of each chicken breast. Make it as deep as you can without cutting all the way through the breast. Place one cheese slice in the slit.

Cut a deep 2-inch-long slit in side of meaty portion of each breast. Slice cheese into 4 equal portions; brush with mustard. Place 1 cheese slice into each slit; secure with wooden picks.

Combine cereal, seasoning, and parsley. Dip chicken in buttermilk; dredge in cereal mixture. Place chicken in a 13- x 9- x 2-inch baking dish coated with cooking spray. Bake at 375° for 1 hour. Yield: 4 servings.

•**Per Serving:** Calories 317   Carbohydrate 27.7g   Protein 35.8g   Fat 6.0g
Fiber 0.3g   Cholesterol 80mg   Sodium 654mg   **Exchanges:** 4 Lean Meat,
1 Starch

Lemon-Herb Roasted Chicken

PREP: 10 MINUTES   COOK: 1 HOUR

1 teaspoon chopped fresh oregano
1 teaspoon chopped fresh rosemary
1 teaspoon chopped fresh thyme
½ teaspoon salt
½ teaspoon pepper
2 cloves garlic, minced
1 (3-pound) broiler-fryer
1 lemon, thinly sliced
  Vegetable cooking spray
  Fresh lemon slices (optional)
  Fresh oregano sprigs (optional)
  Fresh rosemary sprigs (optional)
  Fresh thyme sprigs (optional)

Loosen the skin from the chicken by running your fingers between the meat and the skin. Rub the herb mixture on the meat of the chicken, underneath the skin.

Place the lemon slices over the herb mixture.

Combine first 6 ingredients; set aside. Trim fat from chicken. Remove giblets and neck from chicken; reserve for another use. Rinse chicken under cold water, and pat dry with paper towels.

Carefully loosen skin from body of chicken by running fingers between skin and meat. Rub herb mixture over meat; place lemon slices over herb mixture. Lift wing tips up and over back; tuck under chicken.

Place chicken, breast side up, on a rack in a shallow roasting pan coated with cooking spray. Insert meat thermometer into meaty part of thigh, making sure it does not touch bone. Bake at 375° for 1 hour or until meat thermometer registers 180°. Cover loosely with aluminum foil; let stand 15 minutes. Transfer to a serving platter. If desired, garnish with lemon slices and oregano, rosemary, and thyme sprigs. Remove and discard skin before slicing. Yield: 6 servings.

•**Per Serving:** Calories 171   Carbohydrate 0.6g   Protein 25.7g   Fat 6.6g
Fiber 0.1g   Cholesterol 79mg   Sodium 272mg   **Exchanges:** 3 Lean Meat

Lemon-Herb Roasted Chicken

Sweet-and-Sour Chicken

PREP: 30 MINUTES   COOK: 40 MINUTES

½ cup pineapple-orange marmalade
1 tablespoon orange-honey mustard
1 tablespoon low-sodium soy sauce
½ teaspoon salt
½ teaspoon minced garlic
8 small chicken thighs (about 1½ pounds), skinned
  Vegetable cooking spray
2 cups cooked long-grain rice (cooked without salt or fat)
1 teaspoon grated orange rind
  Kiwifruit slices (optional)
  Orange slices (optional)

Combine first 5 ingredients in a small saucepan. Cook over low heat until marmalade melts; remove from heat, and set aside.

Place chicken in a 13- x 9- x 2-inch baking dish coated with cooking spray. Bake, uncovered, at 450° for 10 minutes. Pour marmalade mixture over chicken; cover and bake at 350° for 30 to 35 minutes or until chicken is done.

Combine rice and orange rind. Spoon ½ cup rice mixture onto each serving plate. Place 2 chicken thighs over rice on each plate; spoon marmalade mixture in baking dish evenly over chicken. If desired, garnish with kiwifruit slices and orange slices. Yield: 4 servings.

•**Per Serving**: Calories 378   Carbohydrate 54.6g   Protein 24.4g   Fat 4.8g Fiber 0.5g   Cholesterol 95mg   Sodium 544mg   **Exchanges**: 3 Lean Meat, 1½ Starch, 2½ Fruit

Sweet-and-Sour Chicken

Citrus Chicken
with Roasted Corn Relish

PREP: 10 MINUTES   MARINATE: 1 HOUR   COOK: 40 MINUTES

4 (6-ounce) skinned chicken breast halves
⅔ cup fresh lime juice, divided
½ teaspoon ground cumin
½ teaspoon chili powder
¼ teaspoon salt
¼ teaspoon ground red pepper, divided
    Olive oil-flavored vegetable cooking spray
1 (16-ounce) package frozen corn with peppers and onions,
    thawed
2 tablespoons chopped fresh cilantro
    Fresh cilantro sprigs (optional)

Place chicken in a heavy-duty, zip-top plastic bag. Reserve 1 tablespoon lime juice; pour remaining juice over chicken. Seal bag; shake to coat chicken. Marinate in refrigerator 1 hour; turn bag occasionally.

Combine cumin, chili powder, salt, and ⅛ teaspoon red pepper in a small bowl. Remove chicken from marinade, discarding marinade. Sprinkle chicken with cumin mixture.

Coat rack of a broiler pan with cooking spray. Place chicken, skinned sides down, on rack; broil 8 inches from heat (with electric oven door partially opened) 25 minutes. Turn chicken, and broil 15 additional minutes or until done. Set chicken aside, and keep warm.

Coat a large nonstick skillet with cooking spray; place over medium-high heat until hot. Add corn mixture and remaining ⅛ teaspoon pepper; sauté until corn is lightly browned and tender. Spoon corn mixture onto individual serving plates; top with chicken. Drizzle with reserved 1 tablespoon lime juice; sprinkle with chopped cilantro. Garnish with cilantro sprigs, if desired. Yield: 4 servings.

•**Per Serving**: Calories 237   Carbohydrate 20.2g   Protein 29.1g   Fat 4.1g
Fiber 1.5g   Cholesterol 72mg   Sodium 226mg   **Exchanges**: 4 Very Lean
Meat, 1½ Starch, 1 Vegetable

Citrus Chicken with Roasted Corn

Cordon Bleu Casserole

PREP: 15 MINUTES   COOK: 45 MINUTES

6 (4-ounce) skinned, boned chicken breast halves
  Butter-flavored vegetable cooking spray
3 (1-ounce) slices reduced-fat, low-salt ham, cut in half
3 (1¼-ounce) slices reduced-fat Swiss cheese, cut in half
2 cups sliced fresh mushrooms
1 (10¾-ounce) can reduced-fat, reduced-sodium
    cream of mushroom soup
3 tablespoons dry sherry
1½ cups reduced-sodium chicken-flavored stuffing mix

Arrange chicken in a 13- x 9- x 2-inch baking dish coated with cooking spray. Top chicken with ham and cheese.

Coat a nonstick skillet with cooking spray; place over medium-high heat until hot. Add mushrooms; sauté until tender. Combine mushrooms, soup, and sherry. Spoon mixture over chicken. Top with stuffing mix; coat well with cooking spray. Bake at 350° for 45 minutes. Yield: 6 servings.

•**Per Serving**: Calories 304   Carbohydrate 20.7g   Protein 38.0g   Fat 8.0g
Fiber 1.4g   Cholesterol 91mg   Sodium 665mg   **Exchanges**: 4 Lean Meat,
1 Starch

*When mushrooms are sautéed, their flavor concentrates and
deepens to become earthy and rich. As you select fresh mushrooms,
look for the whitest ones (they darken with age).*

Chicken with Creole Cabbage

PREP: 15 MINUTES   COOK: 15 MINUTES

4 (4-ounce) skinned, boned chicken breast halves
¼ teaspoon salt
¼ teaspoon black pepper
  Butter-flavored vegetable cooking spray
3 cups coarsely chopped cabbage
¼ cup water
½ teaspoon sugar
¼ teaspoon ground red pepper
⅛ teaspoon ground allspice
1 clove garlic, minced
1 (15-ounce) can tomato sauce with onion, green peppers, and celery

Sprinkle chicken with salt and ¼ teaspoon black pepper. Coat a large nonstick skillet with cooking spray; place over medium-high heat until hot. Add chicken, and cook 3 to 5 minutes on each side or until browned. Remove chicken from skillet. Add cabbage and remaining 6 ingredients to skillet; stir well.

Place chicken over cabbage mixture. Bring to a boil; cover, reduce heat, and simmer 15 minutes or until chicken is done and cabbage is tender, stirring occasionally. Yield: 4 servings.

•Per Serving: Calories 177 Carbohydrate 10.5g Protein 27.7g Fat 2.6g Fiber 2.1g Cholesterol 66mg Sodium 474mg Exchanges: 3 Very Lean Meat, 2 Vegetable

Turkey French Bread Pizzas

PREP: 23 MINUTES   COOK: 5 MINUTES

Vegetable cooking spray
1½ pounds freshly ground raw turkey breast
1½ cups sliced fresh mushrooms
¾ cup chopped onion
1 clove garlic, crushed
1 (15-ounce) can pizza sauce
⅛ teaspoon salt
2 (8-ounce) loaves French bread
1½ cups (6 ounces) shredded part-skim mozzarella cheese

Coat a large nonstick skillet with cooking spray, and place over medium-high heat until hot. Add turkey and next 3 ingredients. Cook until turkey is browned, stirring until it crumbles. Drain, if necessary. Stir in pizza sauce and salt; cook until thoroughly heated.

Cut each loaf in half horizontally; cut each horizontal piece in half crosswise. Place on an ungreased baking sheet, cut sides up. Broil 5½ inches from heat (with electric oven door partially opened) 1 minute or until lightly toasted. Spoon turkey mixture over French bread pieces; sprinkle with cheese. Broil 5½ inches from heat until cheese melts. Yield: 8 servings.

•**Per Serving**: Calories 355   Carbohydrate 37.6g   Protein 30.7g   Fat 8.4g   Fiber 3.0g   Cholesterol 56mg   Sodium 638mg   **Exchanges**: 3 Lean Meat, 2 Starch, 1 Vegetable

Turkey Tenderloins
with Black Bean Salsa

PREP: 12 MINUTES   MARINATE: 20 MINUTES   COOK: 16 MINUTES

1 (15-ounce) can no-salt-added black beans, drained
1 cup no-salt-added salsa
½ cup fresh lime juice
½ teaspoon ground red pepper
½ teaspoon ground cumin
¼ teaspoon salt
4 cloves garlic, crushed
2 (½-pound) turkey tenderloins
   Vegetable cooking spray

Combine black beans and salsa, stirring well. Cover and chill.

Combine lime juice and next 4 ingredients in a heavy-duty, zip-top plastic bag. Add turkey; seal bag, and shake until turkey is well coated. Marinate in refrigerator 20 minutes, turning bag once.

Remove turkey from marinade, reserving marinade. Place marinade in a small saucepan; bring to a boil. Remove from heat, and set aside. Coat grill rack with cooking spray; place on grill over medium-hot coals (350° to 400°). Place turkey on rack; grill, covered, 8 to 10 minutes on each side or until turkey is done, turning and basting with reserved marinade. Cut turkey diagonally across grain into thin slices. Serve with black bean salsa. Yield: 4 servings.

•**Per Serving:** Calories 264   Carbohydrate 24.5g   Protein 33.2g   Fat 3.6g   Fiber 3.2g   Cholesterol 59mg   Sodium 284mg   **Exchanges:** 4 Very Lean Meat, 1½ Starch

Roasted Turkey Breast

PREP: 5 MINUTES   COOK: 2 HOURS

1 (4½-pound) turkey breast
    Vegetable cooking spray
½ teaspoon vegetable oil

Trim fat from turkey. Rinse turkey under cold water, and pat dry. Place turkey, skin side up, on a rack in a roasting pan coated with cooking spray. Brush lightly with oil. Insert meat thermometer into meaty part of breast, making sure it does not touch bone. Bake at 325° for 2 to 2 hours and 30 minutes or until meat thermometer registers 170°. Let turkey stand 15 minutes.

Remove and discard skin from turkey. Remove meat from bones, reserving carcass for other recipes, if desired. Slice turkey into 5 (6-ounce) portions, and place in 5 labeled heavy-duty, zip-top plastic bags. Store in refrigerator up to 1 week or in freezer up to 3 months. Yield: 10 servings.

•**Per Serving**: Calories 142   Carbohydrate 0.0g   Protein 26.4g   Fat 3.1g   Fiber 0.0g   Cholesterol 61mg   Sodium 57mg   **Exchanges**: 3½ Lean Meat

* * * * * * * * * * *

When carving a turkey, start with the proper carving utensils.
You'll need a knife with a very sharp edge, and a large two-tined carving fork.
Hold the bird securely with the fork. Beginning at the meaty area
above the shoulder joint, cut thin slices diagonally through the
meat (across the grain) the entire length of the breast.

Roasted Turkey Breast

Grilled Amberjack with Caramelized Onion

PREP: 9 MINUTES   MARINATE: 30 MINUTES   COOK: 30 MINUTES

¼ cup plus 2 tablespoons reduced-calorie maple syrup, divided
3 tablespoons low-sodium teriyaki sauce
1 tablespoon lemon juice
2 teaspoons minced garlic
6 (4-ounce) amberjack or yellowtail fillets (¾ inch thick)
  Butter-flavored vegetable cooking spray
1 large sweet onion, thinly sliced
2 teaspoons margarine, melted

Combine ¼ cup maple syrup, teriyaki sauce, lemon juice, and garlic in a large heavy-duty, zip-top plastic bag. Add fish. Seal bag, and shake gently until fish is well coated. Marinate in refrigerator 30 minutes.

Coat one side of a 12-inch square of heavy-duty aluminum foil with cooking spray. Place onion slices on half of coated side of foil. Combine remaining 2 tablespoons maple syrup and margarine, stirring well. Drizzle syrup mixture over onion. Fold foil over onion; crimp edges to seal.

Coat grill rack with cooking spray; place on grill over medium-hot coals (350° to 400°). Place foil packet on rack; grill, covered, 20 to 25 minutes or until onion is tender and golden. Set aside, and keep warm.

Remove fish from marinade, reserving marinade. Place marinade in a small saucepan; bring to a boil, and set aside. Place fish on rack; grill, covered, 4 to 6 minutes on each side or until fish flakes easily when tested with a fork, basting often with reserved marinade. Transfer fish to a serving platter; top with onion. Yield: 6 servings.

•**Per Serving**: Calories 147   Carbohydrate 8.6g   Protein 21.5g   Fat 2.8g
Fiber 1.0g   Cholesterol 58mg   Sodium 270mg   **Exchanges**: 3 Very Lean Meat, 1 Vegetable

Greek-Style Flounder

PREP: 7 MINUTES   COOK: 15 MINUTES

¼ cup lemon juice
1½ tablespoons balsamic vinegar
1 teaspoon dried oregano
1½ teaspoons olive oil
¼ teaspoon salt
⅛ teaspoon pepper
4 (4-ounce) flounder fillets
  Vegetable cooking spray
3 tablespoons chopped fresh parsley

Combine first 6 ingredients in a small bowl.

Place fish in a 13- x 9- x 2-inch baking dish coated with cooking spray; pour lemon juice mixture over fish. Bake at 350° for 13 to 15 minutes or until fish flakes easily when tested with a fork. Sprinkle with parsley. Yield: 4 servings.

•**Per Serving**: Calories 115   Carbohydrate 0.9g   Protein 21.5g   Fat 2.4g
Fiber 0.1g   Cholesterol 54mg   Sodium 166mg   **Exchanges**: 3 Very Lean Meat

Italian Red Snapper

PREP: 11 MINUTES   COOK: 25 MINUTES

4 (4-ounce) red snapper fillets
¼ cup dry white wine
¼ cup lemon juice
½ teaspoon dried oregano
½ teaspoon dried basil
¼ teaspoon salt
¼ teaspoon pepper
4 cloves garlic, minced
1 (14½-ounce) can no-salt-added diced tomatoes, drained

Place fish in an 11- x 7- x 1½-inch baking dish. Combine wine and next 6 ingredients, stirring well. Pour wine mixture and tomatoes over fish. Bake, uncovered, at 350° for 25 minutes or until fish flakes easily when tested with a fork. Yield: 4 servings.

•**Per Serving**: Calories 136   Carbohydrate 5.7g   Protein 24.1g   Fat 1.6g
Fiber 0.6g   Cholesterol 42mg   Sodium 229mg   **Exchanges**: 3 Very Lean
Meat, 1 Vegetable

• • • • • • • • • • • • •

If you have fresh herbs on hand,

use 1½ teaspoons each of minced oregano and basil

in place of the dried herbs in this recipe

Hobo Fish Dinner

PREP: 15 MINUTES COOK: 30 MINUTES

Vegetable cooking spray
1 teaspoon salt-free lemon-pepper seasoning
½ teaspoon salt
½ teaspoon dried dillweed
4 small baking potatoes, thinly sliced
3 cups thinly sliced onion (about 2 medium)
1 cup thinly sliced carrot (about 2 medium)
4 (4-ounce) halibut fillets (or any firm white fish)

Coat one side of 4 (18-inch) squares of heavy-duty aluminum foil with cooking spray.

Combine lemon-pepper seasoning, salt, and dillweed. Arrange potato slices evenly in centers of coated foil squares. Sprinkle potato with one-third of seasoning mixture. Place onion over potato; sprinkle with one-half of remaining seasoning mixture. Top with carrot slices, and sprinkle with remaining seasoning mixture. Place fish over vegetables. Fold foil over fish and vegetables; crimp edges to seal.

Place foil packets on a baking sheet. Bake at 450° for 30 to 35 minutes or until fish flakes easily when tested with a fork.
Yield: 4 servings.

•**Per Serving**: Calories 268 Carbohydrate 32.0g Protein 27.8g Fat 3.2g Fiber 5.1g Cholesterol 53mg Sodium 378mg **Exchanges**: 3 Very Lean Meat, 1½ Starch, 2 Vegetable

TECHNIQUE

Layer the vegetables, seasonings, and fish in the center of the aluminum foil.

Fold the foil over the food, and seal tightly.

Glazed Salmon Steaks

PREP: 10 MINUTES   MARINATE: 1 HOUR   COOK: 8 MINUTES

½ cup low-sodium soy sauce
⅓ cup dry sherry
1 clove garlic, crushed
8 (4-ounce) salmon steaks (½ inch thick)
⅓ cup firmly packed brown sugar
2 tablespoons honey
2 teaspoons vegetable oil
  Vegetable cooking spray
  Flowering chives (optional)

Combine first 3 ingredients in a large heavy-duty, zip-top plastic bag. Add fish; seal bag, and shake until fish is well coated. Marinate in refrigerator 1 hour, turning occasionally.

Remove fish from marinade, reserving 3 tablespoons marinade. Discard remaining marinade. Combine reserved marinade, brown sugar, honey, and oil in a small saucepan. Cook over medium heat until mixture comes to a boil and sugar dissolves.

Coat grill rack with cooking spray; place on grill over medium-hot coals (350° to 400°). Place fish on rack. Grill, covered, 4 to 5 minutes on each side or until fish flakes easily when tested with a fork, basting occasionally with brown sugar mixture. Garnish with flowering chives, if desired. Yield: 8 servings.

•**Per Serving:** Calories 248   Carbohydrate 13.3g   Protein 23.3g   Fat 10.6g Fiber 0.0g   Cholesterol 74mg   Sodium 158mg   **Exchanges:** 3 Lean Meat, 1 Starch

Glazed Salmon Steaks

Parmesan-Romano Tilapia

PREP: 6 MINUTES   COOK: 10 MINUTES

¼ cup reduced-fat mayonnaise
1 tablespoon dried onion flakes
2 teaspoons low-sodium Worcestershire sauce
1 teaspoon Dijon mustard
1 teaspoon dry sherry
4 (4-ounce) tilapia fillets (or flounder or orange roughy)
   Vegetable cooking spray
2 tablespoons grated Parmesan-Romano cheese blend

   Combine first 5 ingredients, stirring well. Place fish in an
11- x 7- x 1½-inch baking dish coated with cooking spray. Spread
mayonnaise mixture over fish; sprinkle evenly with cheese. Bake,
uncovered, at 425° for 10 to 12 minutes or until fish flakes easily
when tested with a fork. Yield: 4 servings.

•**Per Serving**: Calories 172   Carbohydrate 2.8g   Protein 22.3g   Fat 7.6g
Fiber 0.1g   Cholesterol 87mg   Sodium 266mg   **Exchanges**: 3 Lean Meat

*No need to open a bottle of sherry for the amount needed in
this recipe. You can use a teaspoon of Sauvignon Blanc instead,
and serve the remainder, chilled, with your dinner.*

Soy-Lime Grilled Tuna

PREP: 10 MINUTES   MARINATE: 30 MINUTES   COOK: 10 MINUTES

 4 (4-ounce) tuna steaks (1 inch thick)
½ cup lime juice
¼ cup low-sodium soy sauce
 1 teaspoon peeled, minced gingerroot
½ teaspoon dried crushed red pepper
   Vegetable cooking spray

Place fish in a shallow baking dish. Combine lime juice and next 3 ingredients, stirring well. Pour lime juice mixture over fish. Cover and marinate in refrigerator 30 minutes, turning fish once.

Remove fish from marinade; reserve marinade. Place marinade in a small saucepan; bring to a boil, and set aside.

Coat grill rack with cooking spray; place on grill over medium-hot coals (350° to 400°). Place fish on rack; grill, covered, 4 to 5 minutes on each side or until fish flakes easily when tested with a fork, basting often with reserved marinade. Yield: 4 servings.

•**Per Serving:** Calories 162   Carbohydrate 0.7g   Protein 25.5g   Fat 5.5g
Fiber 0.0g   Cholesterol 42mg   Sodium 140mg   **Exchanges:** 3 Lean Meat

Spicy Shrimp Creole

Spicy Shrimp Creole

PREP: 20 MINUTES   COOK: 20 MINUTES

1 pound unpeeled medium-size fresh shrimp
  Olive oil-flavored vegetable cooking spray
1 cup chopped onion
1 cup chopped green pepper
½ teaspoon dried crushed red pepper
6 cloves garlic, minced
2 (14½-ounce) cans Cajun-style stewed tomatoes, undrained
5 cups cooked long-grain rice (cooked without salt or fat)

Peel and devein shrimp; set aside.

Coat a nonstick skillet with cooking spray; place over medium-high heat until hot. Add onion and next 3 ingredients; sauté until tender. Add tomatoes. Bring to a boil; reduce heat, and simmer, uncovered, 10 minutes, stirring occasionally. Add shrimp. Cover and cook 5 minutes or until shrimp turn pink. Serve over rice. Yield: 5 servings.

•**Per Serving:** Calories 362   Carbohydrate 66.4g   Protein 20.0g   Fat 1.7g   Fiber 4.8g   Cholesterol 103mg   Sodium 748mg   **Exchanges:** 2 Very Lean Meat, 3 Starch, 5 Vegetable

Citrus Scallop Sauté

PREP: 8 MINUTES   COOK: 8 MINUTES

Vegetable cooking spray
1 ½ teaspoons olive oil
  1 pound sea scallops
  1 (6-ounce) package frozen snow pea pods, thawed
  1 cup diagonally sliced celery
  1 clove garlic, minced
  1 cup unsweetened orange juice
  2 teaspoons cornstarch
  ¼ teaspoon ground ginger
  ⅛ teaspoon dry mustard
  ⅛ teaspoon ground red pepper
  2 medium navel oranges, peeled and sectioned

Coat a large nonstick skillet with cooking spray; add olive oil. Place over medium-high heat until hot. Add scallops, and sauté 2 to 3 minutes. Add snow peas, celery, and garlic; sauté 4 minutes or until vegetables are crisp-tender.

Remove mixture from skillet, using a slotted spoon; set aside, and keep warm. Discard remaining liquid, and wipe skillet dry with a paper towel.

Combine orange juice and next 4 ingredients in skillet, stirring well. Cook over medium heat, stirring constantly, until thickened. Return scallop mixture to skillet. Add orange sections, and heat thoroughly. Yield: 4 servings.

•**Per Serving**: Calories 199   Carbohydrate 22.1g   Protein 21.5g   Fat 2.8g
Fiber 4.3 g   Cholesterol 38 mg   Sodium 209 mg   **Exchanges**: 3 Lean Meat,
1 Vegetable, 1 Fruit

SALADS

Pesto Potato Salad (page 162)

Honeyed Fruit Salad

PREP: 15 MINUTES

¼ cup vanilla low-fat yogurt

2 tablespoons reduced-calorie mayonnaise

1 tablespoon honey

Dash of ground ginger

Dash of ground cinnamon

1½ cups cubed Red Delicious apple

1½ cups cubed ripe pear

1 cup fresh orange sections

¼ cup golden raisins

4 lettuce leaves

Combine first 5 ingredients in a small bowl, stirring well. Combine apple and next 3 ingredients; toss lightly.

To serve, spoon fruit mixture evenly onto 4 lettuce-lined salad plates. Drizzle yogurt mixture evenly over fruit. Yield: 4 servings.

•**Per Serving**: Calories 152   Carbohydrate 33.3g   Protein 1.9g   Fat 2.7g Fiber 5.2g   Cholesterol 3mg   Sodium 68mg   **Exchanges**: 2 Fruit, ½ Fat

Pears are most flavorful when fully ripe. To ripen, place pears in a bowl and leave at room temperature until they yield slightly to gentle pressure. To hasten ripening, place pears in a paper bag. Once ripe, pears should be refrigerated.

Arugula with Sun-Dried Tomatoes

PREP: 14 MINUTES

 8 sun-dried tomatoes (packed without oil)

½ cup hot water

⅓ cup fat-free French dressing

 1 tablespoon balsamic vinegar

 1 tablespoon unsweetened apple juice

 1 teaspoon Dijon mustard

⅛ teaspoon pepper

 4 cups torn arugula

¼ cup freshly grated Parmesan cheese

Combine tomatoes and hot water in a small bowl; let stand 10 minutes. Drain and cut tomatoes into quarters.

Combine dressing and next 4 ingredients in a small bowl, stirring well. Combine tomato and arugula in a bowl, tossing lightly. Drizzle dressing mixture over arugula mixture. Sprinkle with Parmesan cheese. Yield: 4 (1-cup) servings.

•**Per Serving:** Calories 69   Carbohydrate 8.9g   Protein 3.6g   Fat 2.2g
Fiber 1.4g   Cholesterol 5mg   Sodium 317mg   **Exchanges:** 2 Vegetable

Radicchio Salad

PREP: 15 MINUTES

⅓ cup white wine vinegar

⅓ cup water

2 tablespoons chopped fresh chives

1 tablespoon Dijon mustard

1 teaspoon minced fresh oregano

1 teaspoon minced fresh thyme

1 teaspoon olive oil

¼ teaspoon sugar

2 cups torn Bibb lettuce

2 cups torn radicchio

2 cups seeded, chopped tomato

2 tablespoons crumbled feta cheese

4 (1/4-inch-thick) slices purple onion, separated into rings

Combine first 8 ingredients in a jar; cover tightly, and shake vigorously.

Combine Bibb lettuce and remaining 4 ingredients in a medium bowl. Pour vinegar mixture over salad; toss lightly. Yield: 4 servings.

•**Per Serving**: Calories 82   Carbohydrate 11.9g   Protein 3.3g   Fat 2.8g
Fiber 3.0g   Cholesterol 3mg   Sodium 178mg   **Exchanges**: 2 Vegetable, ½ Fat

Radicchio Salad

Snow Pea Salad

Snow Pea Salad

PREP: 11 MINUTES

2 tablespoons rice wine vinegar
1 tablespoon low-sodium soy sauce
¼ teaspoon ground ginger
¼ teaspoon garlic powder
1 cup fresh snow pea pods
1 (8-ounce) can water chestnuts, drained
1 tablespoon chopped fresh parsley
   Green onion fans (optional)

Combine first 4 ingredients in a jar; cover jar tightly, and shake vigorously.

Wash snow peas; remove ends. Arrange snow peas in a vegetable steamer over boiling water. Cover and steam 3 minutes; drain and rinse with cold water.

Combine snow peas, water chestnuts, and parsley in a small bowl. Pour vinegar mixture over snow pea mixture; toss lightly. Garnish with green onion fans, if desired. Yield: 2 servings.

•**Per Serving**: Calories 72   Carbohydrate 14.2g   Protein 3.0g   Fat 0.2g
Fiber 2.5g   Cholesterol 0mg   Sodium 209mg   **Exchanges**: 3 Vegetable

White Bean and Tomato Salad

PREP: 15 MINUTES   STAND: 30 MINUTES

2 (15-ounce) cans cannellini beans
    (or Great Northern Beans), drained
1½ cups chopped tomato
⅓ cup shredded fresh basil
⅓ cup crumbled feta cheese
¼ cup white balsamic vinegar
1½ tablespoons olive oil
½ teaspoon sugar
¼ teaspoon salt
¼ teaspoon freshly ground pepper
    Green leaf lettuce leaves (optional)

Combine first 4 ingredients in a bowl; set aside.

Combine vinegar and next 4 ingredients in a small jar. Cover tightly; shake vigorously. Pour vinegar mixture over bean mixture. Let stand at room temperature 30 minutes, stirring occasionally. Serve on lettuce-lined salad plates, if desired. Yield: 6 (¾-cup) servings.

•**Per Serving**: Calories 142   Carbohydrate 16.4g   Protein 6.1g   Fat 5.6g
Fiber 2.8g   Cholesterol 7mg   Sodium 512mg   **Exchanges**: 1 Starch, 1 Fat

Either regular or white balsamic vinegar will give this salad a great flavor, but the white balsamic won't discolor the beans.

. . . .

Blue Cheese-Green Bean
Potato Salad

PREP: 20 MINUTES

 1 pound small round red potatoes
 1 (10-ounce) package frozen cut green beans
⅓ cup red wine vinegar
 2 teaspoons vegetable oil
 2 teaspoons sugar
¼ teaspoon salt
⅛ teaspoon pepper
¼ cup crumbled blue cheese
 2 slices turkey bacon, cooked and crumbled

Cut each potato into 8 pieces. Cook potato in boiling water to cover 10 minutes. Add beans; cook 5 additional minutes or until potato is tender. Drain well, and place in a large bowl.

Combine vinegar and next 4 ingredients in a small bowl, stirring well. Pour vinegar mixture over potato mixture; toss lightly. Top with blue cheese and bacon. Yield: 6 (¾-cup) servings.

•**Per Serving:** Calories 117   Carbohydrate 17.6g   Protein 4.2g   Fat 3.7g
Fiber 2.7g   Cholesterol 7mg   Sodium 242mg   **Exchanges:** ½ Starch,
1 Vegetable, 1 Fat

Blue cheese is considered a strong-flavored cheese.
That's great for low-fat cooking because you can use just
a little and still get a lot of flavor.

Pesto Potato Salad

PREP: 35 MINUTES

TECHNIQUE

*The easiest way to cut up
sun-dried tomatoes is to use
your kitchen shears.*

½ cup sun-dried tomatoes (packed without oil)
½ cup hot water
2 pounds small round red potatoes
   Olive oil-flavored vegetable cooking spray
½ cup sliced green onions
2 cloves garlic, minced
⅓ cup reduced-fat Caesar dressing
½ cup nonfat sour cream
2 tablespoons pesto
¼ teaspoon freshly ground pepper

Coarsely chop tomatoes. Combine tomato and hot water in a small bowl; let stand 10 minutes. Drain and set aside.

Cut potatoes into 1-inch cubes. Cook potato in boiling water to cover 15 to 17 minutes or until tender. Let cool slightly.

Coat a large nonstick skillet with cooking spray; place over medium-high heat until hot. Add tomato, potato, green onions, and garlic to skillet; sauté 5 minutes. Add dressing, deglazing skillet by scraping particles that cling to bottom. Cook 1 minute; set aside, and keep warm.

Combine sour cream, pesto, and pepper in a large bowl, stirring well. Add potato mixture, and toss lightly until combined. Yield: 6 (1-cup) servings. *(photo on page 153)*

•**Per Serving**: Calories 201   Carbohydrate 32.0g   Protein 6.1g   Fat 5.7g
Fiber 3.8g   Cholesterol 3mg   Sodium 446mg   **Exchanges**: 2 Starch, 1 Fat

Roasted Potato and
Red Pepper Salad

PREP: 15 MINUTES   STAND: 15 MINUTES   COOK: 40 MINUTES

1½ pounds small round red potatoes
1   tablespoon minced fresh rosemary
¼   teaspoon freshly ground pepper
¼   cup reduced-fat olive oil vinaigrette, divided
     Olive oil-flavored vegetable cooking spray
⅓   cup reduced-fat mayonnaise
2   tablespoons freshly grated Asiago (or Parmesan) cheese
1   (12-ounce) jar roasted red peppers, drained, rinsed, and cut into
     1-inch pieces

Cut potatoes into 1-inch cubes. Combine potato, rosemary, and ¼ teaspoon pepper in a large bowl. Add 2 tablespoons vinaigrette; toss well. Let stand 15 minutes.

Place potato mixture in a shallow roasting pan coated with cooking spray. Bake at 400° for 40 to 45 minutes or until potato is tender. Let cool slightly.

Combine remaining 2 tablespoons vinaigrette, mayonnaise, and cheese in a large bowl, stirring well. Add roasted potato mixture and roasted pepper; toss lightly. Yield: 6 (¾-cup) servings.

•**Per Serving:** Calories 156   Carbohydrate 27.8g   Protein 3.4g   Fat 3.8g
Fiber 2.1g   Cholesterol 2mg   Sodium 320mg   **Exchanges:** 1½ Starch,
1 Vegetable, 1 Fat

Pasta-Vegetable Salad

PREP: 15 MINUTES   CHILL: 1 HOUR

6 ounces tricolor fusilli (corkscrew pasta), uncooked
1 (16-ounce) package frozen broccoli, onion, red pepper, and
    mushrooms, thawed
1 (11-ounce) package frozen asparagus spears, thawed and cut
    into 1-inch pieces
1 (9-ounce) package frozen artichoke hearts, thawed
½ cup tomato chutney
½ cup reduced-fat pesto-Parmesan salad dressing (such as Maple
    Grove Farms Lite Pesto-Parmesan dressing)
½ teaspoon freshly ground pepper
½ cup freshly grated Parmesan cheese

Cook pasta according to package directions, omitting salt and fat. Drain; rinse with cold water, and drain again. Place pasta in a large bowl; set aside.

Drain thawed vegetables, and press lightly between paper towels to remove excess moisture. Add vegetables, chutney, dressing, and pepper to pasta; toss lightly. Cover and chill thoroughly. Sprinkle with cheese just before serving. Yield: 7 (1-cup) servings.

•**Per Serving**: Calories 234   Carbohydrate 38.6g   Protein 9.1g   Fat 5.4g
Fiber 2.7g   Cholesterol 4mg   Sodium 338mg   **Exchanges**: 2 Starch,
1 Vegetable, 1 Fat

Create your own variations of this salad by using other

frozen vegetable combinations in similar package sizes.

Black-Eyed Pea and Rice Salad

PREP: 10 MINUTES   COOK: 25 MINUTES

         3 cups water
        ½ cup chopped onion
        ½ cup chopped celery
        ¼ teaspoon salt
        ¼ teaspoon pepper
         4 ounces Canadian bacon, coarsely chopped
         2 (15-ounce) cans black-eyed peas, drained
         1 (10-ounce) package frozen turnip greens, thawed
      1½ cups long-grain rice, uncooked
         1 tablespoon drained, minced hot peppers in vinegar

Combine first 8 ingredients in a large saucepan. Bring to a boil; stir in rice. Cover, reduce heat, and simmer 25 minutes or until rice is tender and liquid is absorbed. Add minced hot peppers; toss well. Serve warm or chilled. Yield: 8 (1-cup) servings

•**Per Serving**: Calories 233   Carbohydrate 42g   Protein 11.3g   Fat 1.9g
Fiber 2.6g   Cholesterol 7mg   Sodium 465mg   **Exchanges**: ½ Lean Meat,
2 Starch, 1 Vegetable

Vegetable-Rice Salad
in Tomato Cups

PREP: 20 MINUTES   STAND/CHILL: 30 MINUTES

6 large tomatoes
3 cups cooked long-grain rice (cooked without salt or fat)
1 (15-ounce) can no-salt-added black beans, drained
1 (10-ounce) package frozen whole-kernel corn, thawed
½ cup chopped purple onion
½ cup reduced-fat olive oil vinaigrette
1 tablespoon chopped fresh cilantro
   Fresh cilantro sprigs (optional)

Cut top off each tomato. Scoop out pulp, leaving ¼-inch-thick shells. Chop pulp to measure 1 cup; reserve remaining pulp for another use. Invert tomato shells on paper towels, and let stand 30 minutes.

While tomato shells stand, combine 1 cup chopped tomato pulp, rice, and next 5 ingredients in a medium bowl. Cover and chill 30 minutes.

To serve, spoon rice mixture evenly into tomato shells. Garnish with fresh cilantro sprigs, if desired. Yield: 6 servings.

•**Per Serving**: Calories 290   Carbohydrate 55.7g   Protein 9.0g   Fat 5.3g
Fiber 6.1g   Cholesterol 0mg   Sodium 179mg   **Exchanges**: 3 Starch,
1 Vegetable, 1 Fat

TECHNIQUE

Cut about ½ inch off the top of each tomato. For a decorative touch, cut a scalloped edge on the top of each cup using a sharp knife.

Scoop out the pulp to make a shell.

Invert the tomato cups on paper towels to drain.

Vegetable-Rice Salad in Tomato Cups

Gingered Pork Tenderloin Salad

PREP: 15 MINUTES   MARINATE: 2 HOURS   COOK: 20 MINUTES

½ cup ginger preserves
⅓ cup rice vinegar
⅓ cup low-sodium soy sauce
1½ tablespoons dark sesame oil
1 (1-pound) pork tenderloin
    Vegetable cooking spray
6 cups shredded napa cabbage (or other Chinese cabbage)
1 cup thinly sliced sweet red pepper

Combine first 4 ingredients in a small saucepan. Place over medium heat; bring to a boil, stirring constantly. Remove from heat, and let cool completely.

Trim fat from tenderloin. Place tenderloin in a heavy-duty, zip-top plastic bag. Pour half of soy sauce mixture over tenderloin; reserve remaining soy sauce mixture. Seal bag; shake until tenderloin is coated. Marinate in refrigerator at least 2 hours, turning occasionally.

Remove tenderloin from marinade, reserving marinade. Insert meat thermometer into thickest part of tenderloin, if desired. Place marinade in a small saucepan. Bring to a boil; remove from heat, and set aside. Coat grill rack with cooking spray; place on grill over medium-hot coals (350° to 400°). Place tenderloin on rack; grill, covered, 20 minutes or until meat thermometer registers 160°, turning and basting occasionally with reserved marinade. Let tenderloin stand 10 minutes; slice diagonally across grain into thin slices.

Combine cabbage and red pepper. Pour remaining half of soy sauce mixture over cabbage mixture; toss lightly. Spoon cabbage mixture evenly onto individual salad plates. Arrange tenderloin slices over cabbage mixture. Yield: 4 servings.

•**Per Serving**: Calories 252   Carbohydrate 24.0g   Protein 25.8g   Fat 6.1g
Fiber 0.9g   Cholesterol 79mg   Sodium 269mg   **Exchanges**: 3 Lean Meat, 2 Vegetable, ½ Fruit

Gingered Pork Tenderloin Salad

Autumn Turkey Salad

PREP: 8 MINUTES   COOK: 15 MINUTES   CHILL: 1 HOUR

1 ½ cups cubed cooked turkey breast

½ cup sliced celery

⅓ cup halved red seedless grapes

1 tablespoon coarsely chopped walnuts, toasted

2 tablespoons nonfat mayonnaise

2 tablespoons low-fat sour cream

1 ½ teaspoons chopped fresh dillweed

1 teaspoon cider vinegar

⅛ teaspoon salt

Combine first 4 ingredients in a small bowl, tossing gently.

Combine mayonnaise and remaining 4 ingredients, stirring well. Add mayonnaise mixture to turkey mixture, and toss lightly to combine. Cover and chill. Yield: 2 servings.

•**Per Serving**: Calories 209   Carbohydrate 9.8g   Protein 27.0g   Fat 6.6g Fiber 1.1g   Cholesterol 64mg   Sodium 411mg   **Exchanges**: 3½ Lean Meat, 1 Vegetable, ½ Fruit

For convenient cooked turkey breast, freeze leftover turkey

from your holiday dinners or prepare Roasted Turkey Breast (page 140).

To freeze cooked turkey, place in air-tight freezer bags or plastic

containers and freeze up to 3 months.

Crab-Papaya Salad

PREP: 20 MINUTES   CHILL: 1 HOUR

 1 pound fresh lump crabmeat, drained
½ cup chopped sweet red pepper
⅓ cup reduced-fat mayonnaise
¼ cup chopped green onions
¼ cup mango chutney
1½ tablespoons horseradish mustard
¼ teaspoon freshly ground pepper
 3 small papayas, peeled, cut in half lengthwise, and seeded
   Green leaf lettuce leaves (optional)

Combine first 7 ingredients in a small bowl, stirring well. Cover and chill.

To serve, spoon ½ cup crab mixture into each papaya half. Place papaya halves on individual lettuce-lined salad plates, if desired. Yield: 6 servings.

•**Per Serving**: Calories 202   Carbohydrate 23.2g   Protein 15.3g   Fat 5.2g
Fiber 2.4g   Cholesterol 75mg   Sodium 478mg   **Exchanges**: 2 Lean Meat,
1½ Fruit

Papayas come in many varieties, sizes, and colors.
The most common type has a green or gold-colored skin
and a sweet perfume-like smell.

Thai Shrimp and Pasta Salad

Thai Shrimp and Pasta Salad

PREP: 30 MINUTES

6 ounces farfalle (bow tie pasta), uncooked
1 pound unpeeled medium-size fresh shrimp
2 teaspoons hot chile oil
2 teaspoons commercial roasted minced garlic
½ cup low-fat spicy Indonesian dressing
1 cup green pepper strips
¼ teaspoon freshly ground pepper
1 (15-ounce) can straw mushrooms, drained
Lime wedges (optional)

Cook pasta according to package directions, omitting salt and fat. Drain; rinse with cold water, and drain again. Place pasta in a large bowl; set aside.

Peel and devein shrimp. Heat oil in a large nonstick skillet over medium-high heat until hot. Add shrimp and garlic; sauté 3 minutes or until shrimp turn pink. Add dressing to skillet, deglazing skillet by scraping particles that cling to bottom. Stir in green pepper, ground pepper, and mushrooms. Bring to a boil; reduce heat, and simmer, uncovered, 2 minutes.

Add shrimp mixture to pasta; toss lightly. Serve warm or chilled. Garnish with lime wedges, if desired. Yield: 4 (1½-cup) servings.

•**Per Serving**: Calories 322   Carbohydrate 39.6g   Protein 25.0g   Fat 7.2g   Fiber 1.3g   Cholesterol 129mg   Sodium 533mg   **Exchanges**: 3 Very Lean Meat, 1½ Starch, 2 Vegetable, 1 Fat

Scallop and Watercress Salad

Vegetable cooking spray
1 pound sea scallops
1 cup sweet red pepper strips
2 cloves garlic, minced
¼ cup plus 2 tablespoons reduced-fat olive oil vinaigrette
1 tablespoon lemon juice
5 cups torn Bibb lettuce
1 cup tightly packed watercress leaves
½ teaspoon freshly ground pepper

Coat a large cast-iron skillet with cooking spray; place over high heat until hot. Add scallops; cook 2 minutes on each side or until browned. Remove scallops from skillet; set aside, and keep warm.

Coat skillet with cooking spray. Place over medium-high heat until hot. Add pepper strips and garlic; sauté 2 minutes or until tender. Add vinaigrette and lemon juice, deglazing skillet by scraping particles that cling to bottom. Cook 1 minute. Return scallops to skillet, and cook until thoroughly heated.

Combine lettuce and watercress in a large bowl. Add scallop mixture to lettuce mixture; toss lightly. Sprinkle with ½ teaspoon pepper. Yield: 4 (1¼-cup) servings.

•**Per Serving**: Calories 165 Carbohydrate 8.5g Protein 20.0g Fat 5.9g Fiber 1.0g Cholesterol 37mg Sodium 369mg **Exchanges**: 3 Very Lean Meat, 1 Vegetable, ½ Fat

SIDE DISHES

Penne with Three Peppers (page 183)

Portobello Mushroom Barley

PREP: 17 MINUTES   COOK: 21 MINUTES

1	small leek (about ¼ pound)
	Olive oil-flavored vegetable cooking spray
1	teaspoon olive oil
5	ounces fresh portobello mushrooms, chopped
1	clove garlic, minced
1	cup quick-cooking barley, uncooked
1⅔	cups canned no-salt-added beef broth, undiluted
⅓	cup dry white wine
⅛	teaspoon salt
2	tablespoons grated Parmesan cheese

Remove and discard root, tough outer leaves, and top from leek. Finely chop leek.

Coat a large nonstick skillet with cooking spray; add oil. Place over medium heat until hot. Add chopped leek, mushrooms, and garlic; sauté until mushrooms are tender. Add barley and next 3 ingredients; bring to a boil. Cover, reduce heat, and simmer 16 to 18 minutes or until barley is tender and most of liquid is absorbed. Remove from heat; let stand 5 minutes. Sprinkle with cheese, and serve immediately. Yield: 5 (¾-cup) servings.

•**Per Serving**: Calories 118   Carbohydrate 20.9g   Protein 4.0g   Fat 2.0g
Fiber 4.0g   Cholesterol 2mg   Sodium 102mg   **Exchanges**: 1 Starch,
1 Vegetable

Portobello mushrooms are large, dark brown mushrooms.
When cooked, they have a rich "meaty" flavor and texture.

Veggie Couscous

PREP: 10 MINUTES   COOK: 10 MINUTES

    Vegetable cooking spray
½ cup diced carrot
½ cup chopped onion
 1 (9-ounce) package frozen cut green beans, thawed
 1 cup canned vegetable broth, undiluted
½ cup water
¼ teaspoon salt
 1 cup couscous, uncooked
 2 tablespoons fat-free Italian dressing

    Coat a nonstick skillet with cooking spray; place over medium-
high heat until hot. Add carrot, onion, and beans; sauté until tender.

    Combine broth, water, and salt in a small saucepan; bring to a
boil. Remove from heat. Add couscous; cover and let stand 5 minutes
or until couscous is tender and liquid is absorbed. Fluff couscous with
a fork. Add vegetable mixture and Italian dressing; toss lightly. Yield:
6 (1-cup) servings.

•**Per Serving:** Calories 134   Carbohydrate 28.3g   Protein 4.7g   Fat 0.7g
Fiber 3.3g   Cholesterol 0mg   Sodium 335mg   **Exchanges:** 1½ Starch,
1 Vegetable

Wild Rice-Vegetable Medley

PREP: 10 MINUTES   COOK: 15 MINUTES

Olive oil-flavored vegetable cooking spray
2 teaspoons olive oil
1 cup chopped green pepper
¾ cup chopped onion
¾ cup finely chopped carrot
1 (8-ounce) package sliced fresh mushrooms
1 (2¾-ounce) package instant wild rice, uncooked
1⅓ cups canned no-salt-added chicken broth, undiluted
¼ teaspoon salt
¼ teaspoon pepper
Fresh flat-leaf parsley leaves (optional)

Coat a saucepan with cooking spray; add oil. Place over medium-high heat until hot. Add green pepper and next 3 ingredients; sauté until carrot is tender. Add rice and broth.

Bring mixture to a boil; reduce heat. Simmer, uncovered, 5 minutes or until liquid is absorbed. Stir in salt and pepper. Let stand 5 minutes. Garnish with parsley, if desired. Yield: 5 (¾-cup) servings.

•**Per Serving:** Calories 157   Carbohydrate 22.4g   Protein 4.1g   Fat 2.6g
Fiber 3.1g   Cholesterol 0mg   Sodium 128mg   **Exchanges:** 1 Starch,
1 Vegetable, 1 Fat

Wild Rice-Vegetable Medley

Mexican Rice Casserole

PREP: 10 MINUTES   COOK: 55 MINUTES

 2 cups water
 1 cup long-grain rice, uncooked
¼ cup skim milk
⅛ teaspoon salt
 1 (10¾-ounce) can reduced-sodium, reduced-fat cream of
     mushroom soup
 1 (4½-ounce) can chopped green chiles, drained
1½ cups (6 ounces) shredded reduced-fat Monterey Jack cheese,
     divided
     Vegetable cooking spray
⅛ teaspoon paprika

Place water in a saucepan; bring to a boil. Stir in rice. Cover, reduce heat, and simmer 20 minutes or until rice is tender and liquid is absorbed. Add milk and next 3 ingredients; stir. Stir in 1 cup cheese.

Spoon mixture into an 11- x 7- x 1½-inch baking dish coated with cooking spray. Cover and bake at 350° for 30 minutes. Uncover and sprinkle with remaining ½ cup cheese and paprika. Bake 5 additional minutes. Yield: 8 (½-cup) servings.

•**Per Serving:** Calories 175   Carbohydrate 22.8g   Protein 8.9g   Fat 5.2g   Fiber 0.7g   Cholesterol 17mg   Sodium 374mg   **Exchanges:** 1 Low-Fat Meat, 1½ Starch

Orange Rice Pilaf

PREP: 10 MINUTES   COOK: 20 MINUTES

1   teaspoon olive oil
¼   cup chopped onion
1   cup long-grain rice, uncooked
1   cup canned no-salt-added chicken broth, undiluted
1   cup unsweetened orange juice
½   cup golden raisins
1   tablespoon grated orange rind
¼   teaspoon salt
¼   teaspoon freshly ground pepper

Heat oil in a medium nonstick skillet. Add onion; sauté until tender. Add rice to skillet; stir well. Cook, stirring constantly, 2 minutes.

Add broth, juice, and raisins. Bring to a boil; cover, reduce heat, and simmer 20 to 25 minutes or until rice is tender and liquid is absorbed. Add orange rind, salt, and pepper; toss lightly. Yield: 5 (¾-cup) servings.

•**Per Serving**: Calories 223   Carbohydrate 49.8g   Protein 3.8g   Fat 1.3g
Fiber 1.5g   Cholesterol 0mg   Sodium 123mg   **Exchanges**: 2 Starch, 1 Fruit

To grate orange rind, rub the outside of a freshly washed
orange against a grater, using firm pressure and quick downward strokes.
Grate only the bright orange part of the rind, stopping before you get
to the bitter-tasting white inner membrane.

Pesto Gemelli

PREP: 4 MINUTES   COOK: 14 MINUTES

2   tablespoons all-purpose flour
¾   cup evaporated skimmed milk, divided
¼   cup dry white wine
2   tablespoons pesto
¼   teaspoon salt
¼   teaspoon cracked pepper
6   ounces gemelli (small pasta twists), uncooked
1½ tablespoons freshly grated Parmesan cheese

Combine flour and ¼ cup milk in a small saucepan, stirring until smooth. Gradually add remaining ½ cup milk and wine. Cook over medium heat, stirring constantly, until thickened and bubbly. Add pesto, salt, and pepper, stirring well.

Cook pasta according to package directions, omitting salt and fat; drain. Add pesto mixture; toss well. Sprinkle with cheese. Yield: 6 (½-cup) servings.

•**Per Serving**: Calories 176   Carbohydrate 28.0g   Protein 7.5g   Fat 3.5g
Fiber 1.0g   Cholesterol 3mg   Sodium 217mg   **Exchanges**: 1½ Starch, 1 Fat

Fresh basil is the main ingredient in pesto. You can store leftover pesto in the freezer in ice cube trays. It will darken a bit in the freezer, but the flavor won't change. Then thaw it to use to spread on bread, tomato slices, fish, and potatoes, or to mix with pasta.

Penne with Three Peppers

PREP: 17 MINUTES   COOK: 5 MINUTES

10 ounces penne (short tubular pasta), uncooked
    Vegetable cooking spray
 1 large sweet red pepper, seeded and cut into 4 pieces
 1 large sweet yellow pepper, seeded and cut into 4 pieces
 1 large green pepper, seeded and cut into 4 pieces
⅓ cup fat-free balsamic vinaigrette
 1 (15-ounce) can cannellini beans, drained
½ cup crumbled feta cheese
    Fresh basil sprigs (optional)

Cook pasta according to package directions, omitting salt and fat; drain. Place pasta in a large serving bowl. Set aside, and keep warm.

Place pepper pieces on a baking sheet coated with cooking spray. Broil 3 inches from heat (with electric oven door partially opened) 5 to 6 minutes or until tender, turning once. Cut peppers into 1-inch pieces.

Add peppers, vinaigrette, beans, and cheese to pasta; toss well. Garnish with fresh basil sprigs, if desired. Yield: 8 (1-cup) servings. *(photo on page 175)*

•**Per Serving:** Calories 211   Carbohydrate 38.3g   Protein 7.8g   Fat 2.6g
Fiber 3.2g   Cholesterol 6mg   Sodium 329mg   **Exchanges:** 2 Starch,
1 Vegetable, ½ Fat

Asian Noodles

PREP: 8 MINUTES   COOK: 4 MINUTES   CHILL: 2 HOURS

3 quarts water
1 (7-ounce) package rice vermicelli, uncooked
3 tablespoons low-sodium soy sauce
2 tablespoons honey
2 teaspoons dark sesame oil, divided
  Vegetable cooking spray
1 cup diagonally sliced green onions
1 tablespoon peeled, minced gingerroot
1 teaspoon toasted sesame seeds

Bring 3 quarts water to a boil in a large saucepan; add pasta, and cook 3 minutes or until tender. Drain. Place pasta in a serving bowl.

Combine soy sauce, honey, and 1 teaspoon oil; stir well with a wire whisk. Add soy sauce mixture to pasta; toss well.

Coat a large nonstick skillet with cooking spray; add remaining 1 teaspoon oil. Place over medium-high heat until hot. Add green onions and gingerroot; sauté 1 minute or until tender. Add onion mixture to pasta mixture; toss lightly. Serve warm or chilled. Sprinkle with sesame seeds just before serving. Yield: 8 (¾-cup) servings.

•**Per Serving**: Calories 224   Carbohydrate 44.3g   Protein 4.5g   Fat 3.2g
Fiber 0.2g   Cholesterol 0mg   Sodium 149mg   **Exchanges**: 2½ Starch, ½ Fat

The freshest gingerroot has smooth skin; wrinkled skin
means the root is old and the flesh will be dry.

Brussels Sprouts with Cheese Sauce

PREP: 12 MINUTES   COOK: 15 MINUTES

36 small fresh brussels sprouts (about 1½ pounds)
1½ cups water
  1 tablespoon reduced-calorie margarine
  1 tablespoon plus 1 teaspoon all-purpose flour
½ cup skim milk
  2 (¾-ounce) slices low-fat process Swiss cheese, cut into strips
    Dash of dry mustard

Wash brussels sprouts thoroughly, and remove discolored leaves. Using a sharp knife, cut off stem ends, and cut a shallow X in bottom of each sprout. Bring water to a boil in a medium saucepan; add brussels sprouts. Cover, reduce heat, and simmer 12 minutes or until brussels sprouts are tender. Drain and keep warm.

Melt margarine in a small heavy saucepan over low heat; add flour, stirring until smooth. Cook, stirring constantly, 1 minute. Gradually add milk; cook over medium heat, stirring constantly, until mixture is thickened and bubbly. Add cheese and mustard, stirring until cheese melts. Spoon sauce over warm brussels sprouts. Yield: 4 servings.

•**Per Serving**: Calories 102   Carbohydrate 14.4 g   Protein 7.9 g   Fat 2.6 g   Fiber 5.1g   Cholesterol 1 mg   Sodium 203 mg   **Exchanges**: ½ Lean Meat, 1 Starch

Nutty Asparagus

Nutty Asparagus

PREP: 6 MINUTES   COOK: 20 MINUTES

  1 pound fresh asparagus spears
     Vegetable cooking spray
  1 tablespoon lemon juice
  2 teaspoons reduced-calorie margarine, melted
1½ tablespoons coarsely chopped walnuts
  ¼ teaspoon salt
  ⅛ teaspoon freshly ground pepper

Snap off tough ends of asparagus. Remove scales from stalks with a knife or vegetable peeler, if desired. Place asparagus in an 8-inch square baking dish coated with cooking spray.

Combine lemon juice and margarine; brush over asparagus. Sprinkle nuts, salt, and pepper over asparagus. Bake, uncovered, at 350° for 20 minutes or until asparagus is tender. Yield: 4 servings.

•**Per Serving**: Calories 48   Carbohydrate 4.5g   Protein 2.6g   Fat 3.0g
Fiber 2.0g   Cholesterol 0mg   Sodium 167mg   **Exchanges**: 1 Vegetable, 1 Fat

Green Beans Parmesan

2 teaspoons reduced-calorie margarine
2 large shallots, sliced and separated into rings
1 pound fresh green beans
1 cup canned low-sodium chicken broth, undiluted
⅛ teaspoon salt
¼ cup freshly shaved Parmesan cheese

Melt margarine in a small nonstick skillet over medium-high heat. Add shallots; cook 20 minutes or until golden, stirring occasionally. Remove from heat, and set aside.

Wash beans; remove ends. Place beans, chicken broth, and salt in a medium saucepan; bring mixture to a boil. Cover, reduce heat, and simmer 12 to 14 minutes or until beans are tender. Drain beans, and stir in shallots. Transfer to a serving dish, and sprinkle with cheese. Yield: 4 servings.

•**Per Serving**: Calories 67   Carbohydrate 8.8g   Protein 3.9g   Fat 2.6g
Fiber 2.3g   Cholesterol 2mg   Sodium 171mg   **Exchanges**: 2 Vegetable, ½ Fat

Green Beans Parmesan

Apricot-Ginger Carrots

PREP: 2 MINUTES   COOK: 20 MINUTES

1 (2-pound) package fresh baby carrots

1 cup water

1 (10-ounce) jar low-sugar apricot preserves

2 tablespoons margarine

2 teaspoons minced crystallized ginger

Combine carrots and water in a medium saucepan; bring to a boil. Cover, reduce heat, and simmer 12 minutes or until carrots are tender. Drain and transfer carrots to a bowl.

Combine preserves, margarine, and ginger in saucepan. Cook over low heat, stirring constantly, 2 minutes or until preserves melt. Return carrots to saucepan; toss lightly. Cook until thoroughly heated. Serve with a slotted spoon. Yield: 10 (½-cup) servings.

•**Per Serving**: Calories 126   Carbohydrate 25.8g   Protein 0.9g   Fat 2.4g Fiber 2.9g   Cholesterol 0mg   Sodium 59mg   **Exchanges**: 1 Vegetable, 1 Fruit, 1 Fat

Crystallized (or candied) ginger has been cooked in a sugar syrup and then coated with coarse sugar. It should be stored in a cool, dry place.

Sesame Sugar Snap Peas

PREP: 15 MINUTES

  Vegetable cooking spray

1 teaspoon dark sesame oil

2 (8-ounce) packages frozen Sugar Snap peas

1 (8-ounce) can sliced water chestnuts, drained

¼ cup low-sodium soy sauce

3 tablespoons brown sugar

1 tablespoon peeled, chopped gingerroot

2 teaspoons cornstarch

Coat a large nonstick skillet with cooking spray; add oil. Place over medium-high heat until hot. Add peas and water chestnuts; sauté 4 to 5 minutes or until peas are crisp-tender.

Combine soy sauce and remaining 3 ingredients, stirring until smooth. Add to vegetable mixture. Bring to a boil, and cook, stirring constantly, 2 minutes or until thickened and bubbly. Yield: 6 (¾-cup) servings.

•**Per Serving**: Calories 90   Carbohydrate 16.7g   Protein 2.4g   Fat 1.1g
Fiber 2.2g   Cholesterol 0mg   Sodium 268mg   **Exchanges**: ½ Starch,
2 Vegetable

*Sugar Snap peas are a cross between English peas
and snow peas. Their thick, crunchy, sweet pods are edible, making
them an easy side dish. Sugar Snap peas can be eaten raw,
or cooked only briefly to retain their crisp texture.*

Baked Butternut Squash

PREP: 5 MINUTES   BAKE: 1 HOUR AND 5 MINUTES

  1 medium butternut squash (about 2 pounds)
⅓ cup mango chutney
  1 teaspoon peeled, grated gingerroot
¼ teaspoon freshly grated nutmeg (or ground nutmeg)

Wash squash; cut in half lengthwise. Remove and discard seeds. Place squash, cut sides up, in an 11- x 7- x 1½-inch baking dish.

Combine chutney, gingerroot, and nutmeg. Brush some of chutney mixture over cut sides of squash; spoon remaining mixture into cavities of squash.

Cover and bake at 400° for 1 hour or until tender. Remove from oven; brush with chutney mixture remaining in dish. Broil 5½ inches from heat (with electric oven door partially opened) 5 minutes or until browned. Yield: 4 servings.

•**Per Serving:** Calories 154   Carbohydrate 39.6g   Protein 2.5g   Fat 0.3g
Fiber 2.8g   Cholesterol 0mg   Sodium 54mg   **Exchanges:** 2 Starch

*Butternut squash is easy to prepare. Once the seeds
are removed, it can be baked, steamed, or simmered until the
orange flesh is tender. Most butternut squash bake in
an hour with no attention required.*

Sweet Potatoes in Orange Syrup

PREP: 15 MINUTES   COOK: 35 MINUTES

2¼ pounds sweet potatoes, peeled and cut into ¼-inch-thick slices
     Butter-flavored vegetable cooking spray
 ¼ cup reduced-calorie maple syrup
  1 tablespoon frozen orange juice concentrate, undiluted
  2 tablespoons coarsely chopped pecans, toasted

Place potato, overlapping slightly, on a jellyroll pan coated with cooking spray. Coat potato with cooking spray. Bake, uncovered, at 375° for 30 minutes or until tender, turning once. Transfer to a bowl.

Combine syrup, juice concentrate, and pecans in a glass measure. Microwave at HIGH 30 seconds; drizzle over potato slices. Yield: 6 (⅔-cup) servings.

•**Per Serving**: Calories 188   Carbohydrate 39.7g   Protein 2.7g   Fat 2.6g
Fiber 4.7g   Cholesterol 0mg   Sodium 22mg   **Exchanges**: 2½ Starch

Pan-Fried Dill Tomatoes

PREP: 18 MINUTES   COOK: 2 MINUTES

1 cup peeled, diced cucumber (about 1 medium)
1 tablespoon cider vinegar
¾ cup fine, dry breadcrumbs
3 tablespoons grated Parmesan cheese
2 tablespoons chopped fresh dillweed
¼ teaspoon freshly ground pepper
⅛ teaspoon salt
2 tablespoons water
2 egg whites, lightly beaten
10 (½-inch-thick) slices tomato (about 3 medium tomatoes)
   Olive oil-flavored vegetable cooking spray

Combine cucumber and vinegar; set aside.

Combine breadcrumbs and next 4 ingredients. Combine water and egg whites, stirring well with a wire whisk. Dredge tomato slices in breadcrumb mixture, and dip in egg white mixture. Dredge in breadcrumb mixture again.

Heavily coat a large nonstick skillet with cooking spray. Place over medium-high heat until hot. Add tomato slices; cook 1 minute on each side or until golden. Serve warm with cucumber mixture. Yield: 5 servings.

•**Per Serving**: Calories 115   Carbohydrate 18.6g   Protein 5.9g   Fat 2.5g
Fiber 2.5g   Cholesterol 2mg   Sodium 282mg   **Exchanges**: ½ Starch,
1 Vegetable, 1 Fat

SOUPS & SANDWICHES

Ratatouille Soup (page 196)

Ratatouille Soup

PREP: 15 MINUTES   COOK: 30 MINUTES

2½ cups peeled, cubed eggplant (about 1 medium)
  2 cups water
  2 (14½-ounce) cans no-salt-added whole tomatoes, undrained and
       chopped
  1 (4-ounce) can sliced mushrooms, drained
  2 cloves garlic, minced
  1 medium zucchini, coarsely chopped
  1 teaspoon dried Italian seasoning
½ teaspoon salt
¼ teaspoon pepper
½ cup freshly grated Parmesan cheese

Combine first 9 ingredients in a Dutch oven, stirring well. Bring
to a boil; cover, reduce heat, and simmer 25 minutes or until vegetables are tender. To serve, ladle soup into individual bowls; sprinkle
evenly with cheese. Yield: 8 (1-cup) servings. *(photo on page 195)*

•**Per Serving:** Calories 63   Carbohydrate 8.4g   Protein 4.3g   Fat 2.0g
Fiber 1.4g   Cholesterol 5mg   Sodium 300mg   **Exchanges:** 2 Vegetable

When selecting an eggplant, look for one that has a dark
glossy color and is pear-shaped, heavy, and firm.

French Onion Soup

PREP: 10 MINUTES   COOK: 30 MINUTES

   Butter-flavored vegetable cooking spray
1 tablespoon reduced-calorie margarine
3 medium-size sweet onions, thinly sliced
3 cups canned no-salt-added beef broth, undiluted
1 tablespoon low-sodium Worcestershire sauce
¼ teaspoon salt
¼ teaspoon pepper
2 tablespoons dry sherry
4 (½-inch-thick) slices French bread, toasted
¼ cup (1 ounce) shredded Gruyère cheese

Coat a Dutch oven with cooking spray; add margarine. Place over medium-high heat until margarine melts. Add onion; sauté 5 minutes or until tender. Add broth and next 3 ingredients. Bring to a boil; cover, reduce heat, and simmer 20 minutes. Stir in sherry.

Ladle soup into individual 2-cup ovenproof bowls; place bowls on a baking sheet. Top each serving with a slice of bread. Sprinkle cheese evenly over bread. Bake at 300° for 10 minutes or until cheese melts. Yield: 4 (1¼-cup) servings.

•**Per Serving**: Calories 221   Carbohydrate 34.4g   Protein 7.3g   Fat 5.5g   Fiber 3.6g   Cholesterol 9mg   Sodium 403mg   **Exchanges**: 1 Starch, 2 Vegetable, 1 Fat

Potato-Broccoli Soup

Potato-Broccoli Soup

PREP: 12 MINUTES   COOK: 25 MINUTES

    3 cups peeled, cubed potato (about 1 pound)
    1 cup frozen chopped broccoli, thawed
    ½ cup chopped carrot
    ½ cup water
    ¼ teaspoon salt
    1 (14¼-ounce) can no-salt-added chicken broth
    1½ cups 1% low-fat milk
    3 tablespoons all-purpose flour
    6 ounces reduced-fat loaf process cheese spread, cubed
      Dried crushed red pepper (optional)
      Dried red chile peppers (optional)

Combine first 6 ingredients in a large Dutch oven. Bring to a boil; cover, reduce heat, and simmer 20 minutes.

Combine milk and flour, stirring until smooth. Add milk mixture and cheese to vegetable mixture in Dutch oven. Cook over medium heat, stirring constantly, until cheese melts and mixture thickens. If desired, sprinkle with crushed pepper, and garnish with a dried red pepper. Yield: 7 (1-cup) servings.

•**Per Serving**: Calories 153   Carbohydrate 22.0g   Protein 9.4g   Fat 3.3g
Fiber 2.0g   Cholesterol 11mg   Sodium 484mg   **Exchanges**: 1 Lean Meat,
1 Starch, 1 Vegetable

Spinach-Chicken Noodle Soup

Spinach-Chicken Noodle Soup

PREP: 5 MINUTES   COOK: 35 MINUTES

4 (14¼-ounce) cans no-salt-added chicken broth
1 cup chopped onion
1 cup sliced carrot
2 (10½-ounce) cans reduced-fat, reduced-sodium cream of
   chicken soup
1 (10-ounce) package frozen chopped spinach, thawed
4 cups chopped cooked chicken (skinned before cooking and
   cooked without salt)
2 cups medium egg noodles, uncooked
½ teaspoon salt
½ teaspoon pepper

Combine first 3 ingredients in a Dutch oven. Bring to a boil;
cover, reduce heat, and simmer 15 minutes. Add cream of chicken
soup and remaining ingredients. Bring to a boil; reduce heat, and
simmer, uncovered, 15 minutes. Yield: 8 (1½-cup) servings.

•**Per Serving:** Calories 227   Carbohydrate 18.9g   Protein 22.0g   Fat 5.9g
Fiber 2.3g Cholesterol 71mg Sodium 388mg   **Exchanges:** 2 Lean Meat,
1 Starch, 1 Vegetable

White Bean Chili

PREP: 10 MINUTES   COOK: 25 MINUTES

Vegetable cooking spray
1 cup chopped onion
1 clove garlic, minced
2 (15-ounce) cans cannellini beans, drained
1 (4-ounce) can chopped green chiles, undrained
2¼ cups canned no-salt-added chicken broth, undiluted
1½ cups chopped cooked chicken (skinned before cooking and cooked without salt)
1 teaspoon chili powder
⅛ teaspoon salt
Nonfat sour cream (optional)
Additional chili powder (optional)

Coat a large saucepan with cooking spray; place over medium-high heat until hot. Add onion and garlic; sauté until tender. Add 1 can beans and next 5 ingredients. Mash remaining can beans with a fork; add to chicken mixture in saucepan. Bring to a boil; cover, reduce heat, and simmer 20 minutes. If desired, top with sour cream and chili powder. Yield: 4 (1½-cup) servings.

•**Per Serving**: Calories 207   Carbohydrate 19.6g   Protein 19.4g   Fat 4.3g
Fiber 3.3g   Cholesterol 43mg   Sodium 554mg   **Exchanges**: 2 Lean Meat,
1 Starch, 1 Vegetable

White Bean Chili

Easy Chicken Gumbo

PREP: 15 MINUTES   COOK: 45 MINUTES

TECHNIQUE

Sprinkle the flour evenly in a jellyroll or baking pan.

Bake the flour at 400° for 10 to 15 minutes or until it's a light brown-caramel color.

¾ cup all-purpose flour
   Vegetable cooking spray
1 (10-ounce) package frozen chopped onion, celery, and
   pepper blend
5 (14¼-ounce) cans no-salt-added chicken broth
2 teaspoons salt-free Creole seasoning
1 teaspoon pepper
½ teaspoon salt
3½ cups chopped cooked chicken (skinned before cooking and
   cooked without salt)
1 (10-ounce) package frozen sliced okra, thawed
4 cups cooked long-grain rice (cooked without salt or fat)

Place flour in a jellyroll or baking pan. Bake at 400° for 10 to 15 minutes or until flour is caramel colored, stirring every 5 minutes. Set aside.

Coat a large Dutch oven with cooking spray; place over medium-high heat until hot. Add vegetable blend; sauté until tender. Sprinkle with browned flour; stir in broth. Add Creole seasoning, pepper, and salt. Bring to a boil; reduce heat, and simmer, uncovered, 20 minutes. Add chicken and okra; cook 20 minutes. Serve over rice. Yield: 8 (1½-cup) servings.

•**Per Serving:** Calories 300   Carbohydrate 39.2g   Protein 21.0g   Fat 4.5g
Fiber 1.1g   Cholesterol 50mg   Sodium 211mg   **Exchanges:** 2 Lean Meat, 2 Starch, 1 Vegetable

Curried Onion and Beef Subs

PREP: 40 MINUTES

Vegetable cooking spray
3 medium onions, thinly sliced
1½ teaspoons curry powder
1 teaspoon commercial roasted minced garlic
4 (2½-ounce) whole wheat submarine rolls
2 tablespoons nonfat mayonnaise
2 tablespoons coarse-grained mustard
½ pound thinly sliced lean roast beef

Coat a large nonstick skillet with cooking spray; place over medium-high heat until hot. Add onion; sauté 5 minutes. Reduce heat to medium-low; cook 20 to 25 minutes or until onion is golden. Stir in curry powder and garlic; cook, stirring constantly, 5 additional minutes.

Cut a ½-inch-thick slice off top of each roll; set tops aside. Hollow out centers of rolls, leaving ½-inch-thick shells. Reserve insides of rolls for another use.

Combine mayonnaise and mustard, stirring well. Spread 1 tablespoon mayonnaise mixture over bottom of hollowed out portion of each roll; top evenly with beef. Spoon onion mixture over beef; cover with tops of rolls. Serve immediately. Yield: 4 servings.

●**Per Serving:** Calories 330   Carbohydrate 46.2g   Protein 19.7g   Fat 7.9g
Fiber 5.5g   Cholesterol 48mg   Sodium 858mg   **Exchanges:** 2 Lean Meat, 2½ Starch, 1 Vegetable

Club Sandwiches

Club Sandwiches

PREP: 15 MINUTES

¼ cup fat-free Thousand Island dressing
8 (1-ounce) slices whole wheat bread, toasted
4 green leaf lettuce leaves
8 slices tomato
4 ounces thinly sliced cooked turkey breast
4 (¾-ounce) slices fat-free sharp Cheddar cheese
4 slices turkey bacon, cooked and cut in half

Spread 1 tablespoon dressing over one side of each of 4 bread slices. Arrange lettuce and remaining 4 ingredients evenly over dressing on slices; top with remaining bread slices. Cut each sandwich into 4 triangles. Secure sandwiches with wooden picks. Yield: 4 servings.

•**Per Serving:** Calories 282   Carbohydrate 38.2g   Protein 21.9g   Fat 4.8g   Fiber 3.3g   Cholesterol 34mg   Sodium 982mg   **Exchanges:** 2 Lean Meat, 2 Starch, 1 Vegetable

Skillet Chicken Pitas

PREP: 5 MINUTES   COOK: 16 MINUTES

TECHNIQUE

Fold left and right sides of pita over the chicken and vegetables to partially enclose the mixture.

Fold the short sides in to form a rectangular package.

Place the sandwiches in the skillet, seam sides down, and cook until lightly browned.

⅓ cup nonfat mayonnaise
¼ teaspoon garlic powder
2 (8-inch) pita bread rounds
6 ounces cooked chicken breast, cut into strips (skinned before cooking and cooked without salt)
1 cup shredded iceberg lettuce
¾ cup chopped tomato
⅓ cup peeled, coarsely chopped cucumber
  Vegetable cooking spray
¼ cup water, divided

Combine mayonnaise and garlic powder. Separate each pita round into 2 rounds. Spread mayonnaise mixture evenly on inside of split rounds. Arrange chicken strips evenly down centers of pita rounds; top evenly with lettuce, tomato, and cucumber. Fold over left and right sides of pita rounds to partially enclose filling. Fold short sides over to form rectangles.

Coat a nonstick skillet with cooking spray. Place over medium-high heat until hot. Sprinkle 1 tablespoon water in skillet. Place 2 sandwiches, seam sides down, in skillet; press firmly. Cook 2 to 3 minutes or until lightly browned. Turn sandwiches; press firmly, and cook 2 additional minutes or until lightly browned. Wrap in wax paper, and keep warm. Repeat procedure. Yield: 4 servings.

•**Per Serving**: Calories 191   Carbohydrate 27.7g   Protein 13.2g   Fat 1.9g   Fiber 4.5g   Cholesterol 29mg   Sodium 600mg   **Exchanges**: 1 Very Lean Meat, 2 Starch

Turkey and Swiss Wraps

PREP: 12 MINUTES   CHILL: 1 HOUR

1 small cucumber
8 (8-inch) flour tortillas
  Dill Aïoli
8 (¾-ounce) slices low-fat Swiss cheese
1 (6-ounce) package low-fat roasted turkey breast
1 cup shredded fresh spinach or lettuce
1 medium tomato, thinly sliced

Peel cucumber; cut in half lengthwise, and remove seeds. Cut each half into ⅛-inch slices.

Arrange 2 tortillas on a flat surface, overlapping edges to form a 12- x 8-inch surface. Spread 1½ tablespoons aïoli over tortilla surface. Place 2 slices Swiss cheese on tortillas, leaving at least a 1-inch border on all sides. Top with one-fourth each of turkey, spinach, cucumber, and tomato. Roll up tightly, beginning at short end. Repeat procedure 3 times with remaining ingredients. Wrap each tightly in plastic wrap, and chill 1 hour. Cut each wrap in half to serve. Yield: 8 servings.

DILL AÏOLI
¼ cup nonfat mayonnaise
1 tablespoon lemon juice
½ teaspoon dried dillweed
1 clove garlic, crushed

Combine all ingredients in a small bowl. Yield: ⅓ cup.

•**Per Serving**: Calories 143   Carbohydrate 19.4g   Protein 11.1g   Fat 2.5g
Fiber 4.5g   Cholesterol 9mg   Sodium 505mg   **Exchanges**: 1 Lean Meat,
1 Starch, 1 Vegetable

Crab Cake Sandwiches

PREP: 20 MINUTES   CHILL: 30 MINUTES   COOK: 8 MINUTES

1 (2-ounce) jar diced pimiento
¼ cup plus 2 tablespoons low-fat mayonnaise
¾ pound fresh lump crabmeat, drained
⅔ cup fine, dry breadcrumbs, divided
¼ teaspoon pepper
1 egg white
   Vegetable cooking spray
4 green leaf lettuce leaves
4 reduced-calorie whole wheat hamburger buns

Drain pimiento, and press between paper towels to remove excess moisture. Combine pimiento and mayonnaise, stirring well. Combine 2 tablespoons pimiento mixture, crabmeat, ⅓ cup breadcrumbs, pepper, and egg white in a bowl; stir lightly. Set remaining pimiento mixture aside.

Shape crabmeat mixture into 4 (¾-inch-thick) patties. Dredge patties in remaining ⅓ cup breadcrumbs. Place patties on a baking sheet; cover and chill 30 minutes.

Coat a large nonstick skillet with cooking spray; place over medium heat until hot. Add patties, and cook 4 minutes on each side or until lightly browned.

Place 1 lettuce leaf on bottom half of each bun; top with crab cakes. Spread remaining pimiento mixture evenly over crab cakes. Top with remaining bun halves. Serve immediately. Yield: 4 servings.

•**Per Serving**: Calories 260   Carbohydrate 38.3g   Protein 21.3g   Fat 4.2g   Fiber 5.8g   Cholesterol 71mg   Sodium 790mg   **Exchanges**: 2 Very Lean Meat, 2½ Starch

Crab Cake Sandwiches

Ham and Mushroom Melt

PREP: 20 MINUTES   COOK: 2 MINUTES

1   (8-ounce) loaf French bread
1   large clove garlic, split
½   teaspoon freshly ground pepper
    Olive oil-flavored vegetable cooking spray
2   teaspoons reduced-calorie margarine
2   (8-ounce) packages sliced fresh mushrooms
4   ounces thinly sliced reduced-fat, low-salt ham, cut into thin
      strips
½   teaspoon chopped fresh thyme
3   ounces provolone cheese, thinly sliced

Cut bread in half horizontally. Rub garlic over cut sides of bread; sprinkle with pepper. Place on a baking sheet, cut sides up. Broil 5½ inches from heat (with electric oven door partially opened) 3 minutes.

Coat a nonstick skillet with cooking spray; add margarine. Place over medium-high heat until margarine melts. Add mushrooms; sauté 8 minutes. Arrange mushrooms over bread; top with ham. Sprinkle with thyme; top with cheese. Broil 5½ inches from heat 2 minutes or until cheese melts. Cut each bread half into 2 pieces. Yield: 4 servings.

•**Per Serving**: Calories 313   Carbohydrate 37.9g   Protein 18.1g   Fat 9.9g
Fiber 2.9g   Cholesterol 30mg   Sodium 757mg   **Exchanges**: 2 Lean Meat,
2 Starch, 1 Vegetable

Grilled Eggplant Sandwiches

PREP: 10 MINUTES   COOK: 18 MINUTES

2 medium eggplants (about 2 pounds)

2 medium-size sweet red peppers

2 small zucchini

   Vegetable cooking spray

⅓ cup fat-free Italian dressing

¼ cup drained, sliced pepperoncini peppers

4 (1-ounce) slices part-skim mozzarella cheese

TECHNIQUE

Cut 2 (½-inch-thick) slices from the opposite lengthwise sides of the eggplant. (These slices have a rounded skin edge and won't work well for the sandwich.)

Cut 2 (½-inch-thick) slices lengthwise from opposite sides of each eggplant; reserve for another use. Cut each eggplant lengthwise into 4 (¾-inch-thick) slices; set aside.

Cut red peppers in half lengthwise; remove and discard seeds and membranes. Flatten pepper halves with palm of hand; set aside. Cut zucchini lengthwise into ¼-inch-thick slices.

Slice the remaining eggplant into 4 lengthwise slices with flesh on both sides.

Coat grill rack with cooking spray; place on grill over medium-hot coals (350° to 400°). Brush eggplant, red pepper, and zucchini with about one-third of dressing. Place red pepper and zucchini on rack; grill, covered, 6 minutes. Turn vegetables, and baste with half of remaining dressing. Add eggplant to grill rack; grill, covered, 10 minutes, turning once, and basting often with remaining dressing.

Arrange pepper halves and zucchini slices evenly over 4 eggplant slices; sprinkle with pepperoncini pepper. Place 1 slice of cheese over each serving. Top with remaining eggplant slices. Grill 2 additional minutes or until cheese melts. Serve immediately. Yield: 4 servings.

•**Per Serving:** Calories 170   Carbohydrate 23.0g   Protein 10.8g   Fat 5.4g
Fiber 5.0g   Cholesterol 16mg   Sodium 438mg   **Exchanges:** 1 Medium-Fat
Meat, 4 Vegetable

Shrimp Louis Boats

PREP: 20 MINUTES   CHILL: 15 MINUTES

3 (2½-ounce) submarine rolls, split
1½ pounds unpeeled medium-size fresh shrimp
1½ quarts water
½ cup nonfat mayonnaise
2 tablespoons chopped green onions
1 tablespoon chili sauce
¾ teaspoon salt-free lemon pepper
12 Bibb lettuce leaves

Hollow out centers of rolls, leaving ½-inch-thick shells. Reserve insides of rolls for another use.

Peel and devein shrimp. Bring water to a boil; add shrimp, and cook 3 to 5 minutes or until shrimp turn pink. Drain well; rinse with cold water. Cover and chill at least 15 minutes.

Combine mayonnaise and next 3 ingredients, stirring well. Stir in shrimp. Line each roll half with 2 lettuce leaves. Spoon shrimp mixture evenly over lettuce. Yield: 6 servings.

•**Per Serving:** Calories 184   Carbohydrate 22.4g   Protein 16.8g   Fat 2.6g
Fiber 0.3g   Cholesterol 124mg   Sodium 644mg   **Exchanges**: 2 Very Lean
Meat, 1 Starch, 1 Vegetable

Shrimp Calzones

PREP: 16 MINUTES   COOK: 18 MINUTES

1 (10-ounce) package refrigerated pizza crust
⅓ cup Italian-style tomato paste
1 tablespoon water
¼ teaspoon dried Italian seasoning
1 (8-ounce) package frozen cooked salad shrimp, thawed and drained
  Butter flavored vegetable cooking spray
1 tablespoon grated Parmesan cheese

Roll pizza crust into an 18- x 10-inch rectangle. Cut into 6 (6- x 5-inch) rectangles.

Combine tomato paste, water, and Italian seasoning. Spread evenly over rectangles, leaving a ½-inch border.

Arrange shrimp evenly over half of each rectangle. Brush edges of rectangles with water. Fold rectangles in half crosswise over shrimp; press edges together with a fork. Place on a large baking sheet coated with cooking spray. Coat tops with cooking spray; sprinkle evenly with Parmesan cheese. Bake at 400° for 18 minutes or until lightly brown. Yield: 6 servings.

•**Per Serving:** Calories 182   Carbohydrate 24.8g   Protein 12.8g   Fat 2.7g
Fiber 1.0g   Cholesterol 74mg   Sodium 370mg   **Exchanges:** 2 Very Lean Meat, 1½ Starch

Metric Conversions

Metric Measure/Conversion Chart
Approximate Conversion to Metric Measures

When You Know...	Multiply by...	To Find...	Symbol
	Mass (weight)		
ounces	28	grams	g
pounds	0.45	kilograms	kg
	(volume)		
teaspoons	5	milliliters	ml
tablespoons	15	milliliters	ml
fluid ounces	30	milliliters	ml
cups	0.24	liters	l
pints	0.47	liters	l
quarts	0.95	liters	l
gallons	3.8	liters	l

Cooking Measure Equivalents

Standard Cup	Volume (Liquid)	Liquid Solids (Butter)	Fine Powder (Flour)	Granular (Sugar)	Grain (Rice)
1	250 ml	200 g	140 g	190 g	150 g
¾	188 ml	150 g	105 g	143 g	113 g
⅔	167 ml	133 g	93 g	127 g	100 g
½	125 ml	100 g	70 g	95 g	75 g
⅓	83 ml	67 g	47 g	63 g	50 g
¼	63 ml	50 g	35 g	48 g	38 g
⅛	31 ml	25 g	18 g	24 g	19 g

Equivalent Measurements

3 teaspoons	1 tablespoon
4 tablespoons	¼ cup
5⅓ tablespoons	⅓ cup
8 tablespoons	½ cup
16 tablespoons	1 cup
2 tablespoons (liquid)	1 ounce
1 cup	8 fluid ounces
2 cups	1 pint (16 fluid ounces)
4 cups	1 quart
4 quarts	1 gallon
⅛ cup	2 tablespoons
⅓ cup	5 tablespoons plus 1 teaspoon
⅔ cup	10 tablespoons plus 2 teaspoons
¾ cup	12 tablespoons

International Ingredient Substitutions

If the following ingredients aren't available in your country, try these ingredient substitutions.

INGREDIENT	SUBSTITUTE OR USE
All-purpose flour	Plain flour
Amberjack fillets	Lean, white fish (usually whole). Substitute any whole white fish.
Arugula or Bibb lettuce	Rocket or roquette (peppery leafy herb)
Black-eyed peas	Pulse, a small cream kidney-shaped bean with a black eye. Available in supermarkets with other canned beans.
Bulgar	Burghal (hulled wheat). Available in Middle Eastern and Greek food stores, health stores, and supermarkets.
Buttermilk (low fat)	For every cup buttermilk: Use 1 cup skim milk yogurt, or 1 cup skim milk with 1¾ teaspoon cream of tartar.
Cajun-style stewed tomatoes	Purchase in supermarket or selected delis. Or add Cajun seasonings to a can of tomatoes.
Canadian bacon	Sugar-cured loin of pork or can be known as smoked pork loin
Cannelli beans	White kidney beans (or similar)
Capellini pasta	Thin, long pasta, usually coiled into nests (like spaghetti)
Cilantro	Fresh coriander
Crimini mushrooms	Large button mushrooms
Ditalini pasta	Short pasta tubes (macaroni)
Egg substitute	Cholesterol-free mix (in freezer section of supermarket)
Farm-raised catfish fillets	White fish (scaleless fish)
Fontina cheese	Substitute Pastorello or Fontinella found in selected delis
French bread dough	May use a Boboli pizza base or a fresh French stick
Hot chile oil	Found in supermarkets, or add chili to oil.
Oyster mushrooms	Found in most Green grocers
Papayas	Found in most Green grocers, or substitute Paw Paw.
Pimiento	Pickled, diced red capsicum (pepper)
Portobello mushrooms	Ordinary mushrooms
Provolone cheese	Similar to mozzarella
Radicchio (torn)	Bitter lettuce
Reduced-fat Monterey Jack	Reduced-fat Cheddar cheese
Reduced-fat loaf process cheese spread	Cheddar sticks or triangles
Roasted minced garlic	Roast fresh garlic, then mince. Or use minced garlic.
Romaine lettuce leaves	Any green lettuce
Round tip steak	Round steak
Salt-free Creole seasoning	Found in spice section of the supermarket
Shiitake mushrooms	Found in most Green grocers
Turkey bacon	Substitute "not quite bacon" found in the dairy section of supermarket (vegetarian section).
Wonton wrappers	Found in any Asian grocer, or substitute spring roll pastry, which is found in supermarkets.

Recipe Index

Subject Index

Acknowledgments

I would like to express my appreciation to an outstanding team of co-workers, business associates and friends who encouraged me to share my views on creating a balanced approach to living and the importance of taking time to tend to your personal needs and fulfillment. Only with their assistance, support and guidance was I able to commit my thoughts to paper as well as deliver this delicious collection of healthful recipes.

To Dianne Mooney for her vision in forging and cultivating a productive partnership with all of our friends at Oxmoor House and Time, Inc.

To Lisa Talamini Jones, R.D. and Cathy Wesler, R.D. for again uniting their creative and culinary expertise as well their professional acumen.

To Ralph Anderson for his wonderful ability to capture on photographic canvas the joy of my daily life as well as the inherent beauty of food.

To Melissa Clark for her artistic genius in integrating a soothing blend of color and graphic elements into this book's design.

To Gary Wright, Brian Luscomb, and Colleen Hanna for their diligence and perseverance in guiding this project through all phases of production, and to Susie Baranowski for her steady support and keen attention to detail.

To the culinary experts in Oxmoor House's test kitchens who spent hours preparing and evaluating all of the recipes featured on the pages of this book.

And to Matisse and Picasso, my faithful canine companions, for their unrequited devotion, and to my new friend Mickey, for enthusiastically returning every ball tossed her way.